How To Collect Art

MAGNUS RESCH

For my father

Foreword
by Pamela J. Joyner

When I reflect upon how I spend much of my time, I hesitate to call myself a collector, an activist, a mission-driven patron, or any of the shorthand monikers commonly used in the art world of this moment. I would prefer to have a readily available term that fully captures the deeply personal and nuanced nature of intensely engaging with art and artists. In the absence of that convenience, I simply affirm that having the ability to spend significant time viewing great art and getting to know gifted and visionary artists is life-enhancing. Of this I am certain.

The ideas that most motivate me along this journey, however, raise issues about which I am materially less clear. I grapple on an ongoing basis with questions around: What role can I play? What are my objectives, and how can I execute them in a way that illuminates the talents of artists?

While I do not have complete answers to these questions, after nearly three decades of searching, I do have a set of experiences, observations, and guiding principles that set the parameters for what will hopefully be my more enlightened next chapters.

If I were beginning my art journey today, after assembling a full library of art books, I would systematically seek out the most talented curators working in museums. I would then spend time with the select few with whom I developed good relationships. Meaningful relationships usually create a level of trust so that one can both ask questions and exchange ideas. Everyone learns from this kind of process.

Without being fully intentional about it, this is essentially what I did in the 1990s and early 2000s when I first began buying art. As a graduate student at Harvard Business School, I met Lowery Stokes Sims, who invited me to learn about and get to know two generations of African American artists whose creative output was brilliantly innovative and insightful. However, race proved to be a systemic and nearly impenetrable barrier for these artists for most of their lives. The survey art history texts did not include many, if any, African American narratives, and while there have certainly been great scholars across the generations, like Lowery, with deep expertise in African American art, they themselves have largely been African Americans who faced the same obstacles as the subjects of their research.

The reality of this environment set the stage early for me to seek partners when advancing my own art education. The key variables for me are scholarship and curatorial insight. I am especially moved by and fortunate to be able to witness leading experts as they do what they do best: create new knowledge. I am a huge beneficiary of their insights and observations. Without those relationships I would not have been able to assemble the works in my collection which tell stories that should be revealed and shared.

For several years, I moved forward in my joyful journey buying art perhaps almost unwittingly because my parents instilled in me a lifelong appreciation of the arts. I was able to identify work, particularly abstraction, that I loved and found personally resonant. Most importantly, I met and spent time with artists who brought to life my romantic notion that they are fascinating people with unusual perspectives on the world. Richard Mayhew, the first artist I got to know personally, was kind enough to introduce me to many talented artists who have shared their stories and artistic brilliance over the years. Richard, who at the time of this writing is in his hundredth year, continues to create, contemplate, and dazzle. I have had the greatest affection and admiration for Richard for more than twenty-five years. My life in a space occupied by creatives would not have unfolded without him. I could not be happier that the art world now seems ready to give Richard the recognition he has long deserved.

Finally, a few years into the 2000s, I began to develop a clear message and execute a group of activities dedicated to illuminating the talents of artists of color so that they could have an opportunity to become etched into the art historical canon. This clarity was a direct result of research I had done and artists I had met who experienced long-term discrimination firsthand. During the same period, many major museums began to question if they had adequately included narratives that fully and fairly represented both local and global communities.

At some point art history will chronicle and evaluate the various catalysts that prompted this environment of change. From my own lived experience, I have a few theories. First, it seems that at roughly the same moment, key art world constituents all embraced some level of change. Certainly, there were initiators and late followers. Scholars will debate who led whom and what motivated the various players. However, real change began to occur when museums, curators, critics, and collectors extended collective and interdependent action to artists of color and other marginalized groups. This was not new behavior. For generations the art ecosystem has held the shared belief that promoting the best of human creativity has urgency and relevance for humanity. The difference now is the system is endeavoring to do so without constructing artificial barriers around race, ethnicity, gender identity, or sexual orientation. This evolution suggests a new set of communal values that resonates intensely for me. Embedded in all of this activity is the notion that it is both necessary and right that the art historical canon be corrected.

Here is where I have sought to play a role. There are a variety of mechanisms available to advance the cause. With an eye toward enhancing the permanent art historical record, I donate art, lend art, provide financial support, and publish books. In addition, I run an artist residency, actively connect people, organize shows of the collection, and buy art on an ongoing basis. I also buy when artists have specific near-term needs.

I am committed to supporting change initiated from the inside of existing institutions, especially with respect to the various museums with which I am involved. At what is perhaps the first moment in history that major institutions are dedicating significant resources to advancing more inclusive narratives, I want to encourage this trajectory, not unravel it.

I take inspiration and counsel from those who have come before me and on whose shoulders I clearly stand. I value the many allies I have met and worked with along the way. Some of these are unlikely people from unexpected places. I do not underestimate the role that serendipity has played in my personal evolution. If I had been ten years older, the environment would not have been open to me, my ideas, and my aspirations for a group of deserving but overlooked artists. If I had been ten years younger, the environment would have become too competitive to enable a clear field of vision.

This book talks about the process of how to collect. One of Magnus's key ideas is the notion of "responsible buying": rather than investing in art to maximize your return, you are supporting artists and their community. I subscribe to this idea. But mistakes will naturally be made. Course corrections will necessarily occur. However, credible, evidenced-based arguments can be made that progress is occurring and that it is likely to be long-term and sustainable. In the broader context, alleviating injustice in one arena creates a roadmap for doing the same elsewhere. The job of rewriting art history is far from complete. My personal view is that I have both an interest in and obligation to play a role in promoting our best collective aspirations. I look forward with enthusiasm.

1
Introduction

—Motivations and Strategies for Collecting

I entered the art market as a young and hopeful (if naive) gallerist twenty years of age, but headlines about the art market have never really changed. Stratospheric prices have led to stories declaring that the market is booming, with the underlying message that, with a little luck, a fortune can be made more easily than in almost any other line of investment. The origin story behind this conviction lies in sensational sales, like da Vinci's *Salvator Mundi*, which was bought for only $1,000 dollars and sold for $450 million—a 450,000-fold increase in fewer than ten years—or the rabbit sculpture by Jeff Koons, which sold for $91.1 million, or the NFT by digital artist Beeple, which sold for $69 million.

The excitement incited by art and the prices it attracts creates overnight superstars in a modern world in which contemporary artist Damien Hirst, who came to the fore with the Young British Artists of the 1990s, has made more money than Picasso, da Vinci, and Monet combined during their lifetimes. Records at auction are broken and broken again, galleries are everywhere, and the aisles of art fairs are packed with stars and celebrities.

1.1 Introduction

None of this, of course, reflects the experience of most people involved in the art market, including the potential buyers for whom I wrote this book. Buying art is not for the faint-hearted. New buyers are overwhelmed by the continual surge of new artists and new forms, by pricing that is arbitrary at best, and by the limited number of brands that can offer a comforting anchor of recognition. To add to this uncertainty, there are no definitive criteria that clarify what "good art," or indeed "bad art," might be. And you will soon realize that throughout the industry, people throw pretty fancy language around about art, with some dazzling insider terminology, but much of it is a bluff, propping up a slender knowledge of both the art and the industry, which is in many ways hard to grasp.

> **Please try to be ahead of your own taste. Quality comes with simple, unpremeditated beauty.**
> Erling Kagge, Collector

Being a new collector in today's art world is tough. And that's why the number of buyers is falling. Every year, fewer and fewer people buy art. Were it not for a few hard-core collectors at the top end of the market who produce record prices, the art market would be in recession. In reality, most galleries close down after only a few years, most artists cannot afford to live from their practice, there are only around six thousand people who spend more than $100,000 per year on art, and pretty much every piece of art that is bought has no resale value whatsoever. Those working on the selling side of the industry, such as gallerists, auction house employees, and art advisors, barely make any money.

> **Collecting art is a journey, and the journey is the reward. So look at everything.**
> Andrea Feldman Falcione, Advisor

In spite of this downbeat picture, there has never been a time when so many people have been interested in buying their first piece of art. This book is all about how to start an art collection. It cuts through the apparent (and, in my view, unnecessary) mystique of the market and breaks down the process of collecting into systematic, logical strategies that cut through the sense that you are navigating uncharted waters.

Develop a strong relationship and collect from a dealer you trust. Take your time—there's no rush. See as much as you can. And understand your taste will change over time.

Mills Morán, Gallerist

If you don't understand how the art market really works, you can spend year after year immersed in it, wasting a small fortune along the way, before sheer experience gives you any real insight. This book—while no substitute for experience—is a shortcut to understanding what really shapes the art market. There are three essential lessons in starting your own art collection:

1

Art is not a good investment, but artists can be. You will learn to identify who those are.

2

Collecting art is fun. I will equip you with frameworks to step confidently into the market on your own.

3

Art buyers are in a really strong position. I will explain how to buy your first piece—without over-spending or a huge budget.

This book is based on almost twenty years of research and practical experience in the art market. I ran a gallery when I was twenty years old, I wrote my PhD in art economics, and I have published seven books to date on the art market, including three bestsellers. I am and have been a professor in art management at prestigious universities around the world—I currently lecture at Yale, but I taught previously at Columbia, the University of St. Gallen, the Luxembourg School of Business, and the Zagreb School of Economics and Management. Finally, I am the founder of two internet art companies: the world's leading art collector database, Larryslist.com, and, with advisor and investor Leonardo DiCaprio, Magnus.net, the company that produced the Magnus artwork-identification app, which works like Shazam for art.

In all these areas of involvement, my approach to the art market is similar:

I rely on data. Although I give due weight to the history, subtleties, and nuances of the art market, I look primarily at market intelligence and the evidence of the bottom line rather than at personal accounts or art historical notes. In a market that has proven to be highly complex, anecdotal evidence has its place but also its limitations. My belief that art is susceptible to economic analysis as much as any other product led me into a six-year project collecting research data on the career history of half a million artists, and an additional three years analyzing the data. The conclusions are discussed in a later chapter; they underpin many of my beliefs about the art market and shape the courses I teach at universities and privately.

If you want to buy something super rare, you need to be ready to pay more than it's worth.
Rüdiger Weng, Collector

I look at the art market from a global perspective. In a market that is so international, an understanding of the wider global context is essential. It is also second nature to me. I live in New York City and spend my winters in Miami, but I was born in Germany, studied at Harvard and the London School of Economics, wrote my PhD in Hong Kong, and lectured in Croatia as well as in Switzerland and the US.

I listen to experts in the field. In my career, I have conducted interviews with more than a thousand art-market professionals. This was invaluable in ensuring that my findings are applicable and verified by leading experts. For this book, I spoke to collectors, private art advisors, gallerists, museum directors, journalists, market researchers, artists, and many others. These conversations with experts in their field helped to generate a bigger picture of the art industry, as well as bring a depth of creativity and diversity to the discussions. You can watch many of these conversations in my online class, magnusclass.com. Some of these have found their way into this book and are presented here as case studies or as pull quotes throughout the text.

Don't buy anything for a specific place. You will find a place for it eventually. Move art around and create a dialogue between pieces. It will inspire you to see things that you would have never believed.

Barbara Levine, Collector

This book offers guidelines to inspire and guide your thinking, but it does not come with a guarantee. Some ideas may not lend themselves to your current position, while others will need adaptation. You have to decide for yourself to what extent my recommendations work for you. You will also come across collectors who have followed a different route to get started in the art market. I do not in any way pretend to have all the answers. In my view, the approach in the following pages is what I intended it to be: accessible, useful, and easily replicated. If nothing else, I hope it will inspire you to buy art with a better sense of your surroundings and the art market.

1.2 Motivations for Collecting

If you want to get the most out of buying art, the best place to start, bar none, is thinking about why you want to buy art. If you can't answer that yet, start with looking at why others buy art. Above all, art is a luxury product. You don't need it, but it's nice to have. A study conducted a few years ago looked at what drives buyers in their pursuit of art ownership.

MOTIVATION TO PURCHASE ART

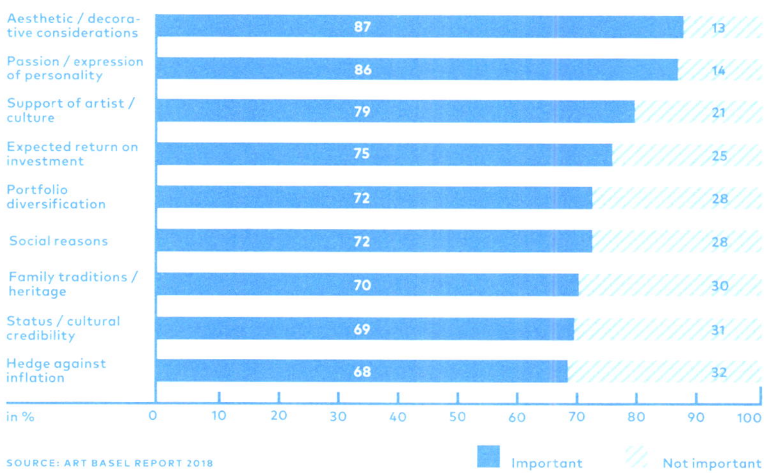

SOURCE: ART BASEL REPORT 2018

As you can see, aesthetic considerations (87%), passion (86%), and support of artists (79%) were the three main drivers, with financial gain ranking only fourth. An interesting variation emerged when we looked at data by country: for Asian collectors, the expected return on investment was considered more important than aesthetic incentives. But in general, if you bought this book because you want something to fill the white space above your sofa, you are not alone. It's the main reason people buy art.

Prominent collections tend to bear out these findings. For example, singer Alicia Keys and her husband, Swizz Beatz, are active collectors. Their Dean Collection focuses on supporting primarily African American artists, including Kehinde Wiley or Mickalene Thomas. John and Vivian Hewitt are another example of collectors of African American artists, enthusiastic about educating and encouraging people to collect. Mega collector Ronald Lauder bought his first artwork at the age of fourteen, a drawing by Egon Schiele. This was the beginning of a lifelong passion for German and Austrian art, leading eventually to the foundation of New York's Neue Galerie, which is devoted to his collection. Or take Herbert and Dorothy Vogel. He was a postal clerk and she a librarian at New York's Brooklyn Public Library. They collected artworks by some of the world's leading artists, such as Sol LeWitt and Richard Tuttle, whose works they bought on Herbert's modest salary. Whatever other criteria they had for collecting, size was paramount: it needed to fit in a New York taxicab so they could take it home. And there is Charles Saatchi, a British marketing-agency owner, who famously turned his professional skills to increasing the value of his personal collection of artworks by emerging British artists fresh from Goldsmiths art school in London in the 1990s. Clever marketing put these artists in the international spotlight, initially framing them as the Young British Artists, which soon turned into a British sensation simply known as the YBAs. Tracey Emin and Damien Hirst are only two of the many artists who reached stardom through Saatchi. And, of course, there are corporate collections, such as the UBS Art Collection. Their goal is often to support artists and help frame the company's culture.

Be patient. Take your time and absorb. Erick Calderon, Collector

Spend a year or more educating yourself and actually go see art at museums, galleries, auction houses, and fairs. When you figure out what sings to you, ignore the background noise and buy what you love! Debi Wisch, Collector

These collectors, and all collectors, each have a personal story and a different motivation. My story as a collector started when I was sixteen. I bought a work by German artist Rupprecht Geiger for 400 deutsche mark (or roughly $200) at a small local auction house in Germany called Sturies Auctions. I bought it simply because I liked it, and I had savings to spend from my job as a shop assistant. But more than buying a piece of art, I was buying an experience and a lifestyle. I was gripped by the atmosphere in the sales room, as I watched art sell for high prices and bidding wars start and end. The scent of deal-making and the elegance of the other buyers all pulled me in. This first piece gave me a taste of not only what it's like to own art but also what the world of art owners could be like.

It's smart to do your research. Learn about the artist, his career, his past auctions, his museum placement, and what galleries represent him. But the golden rule for me is only buy something you love and that moves you personally when you see it. Even if the value is zero dollars, it still makes you smile and makes you happy.

Shaun Neff, Collector

My reasons for collecting have changed, too, over time. At the outset, I was fascinated by the collecting world. Then I became more preoccupied with the aesthetic side, and with choosing art that I loved and wanted to live with in my own home. Today, I get a lot of pleasure from the work itself, but the whole art environment, with the associations and social status that come with the art-collecting scene, is also a factor. And most importantly, I am supporting an artist and the community that comes with her. I call it responsible buying—the notion that buying art is not just an exchange of monetary value but also a philanthropic act. Far from putting money into an asset, I donate it, knowing that in all likelihood I won't be able to resell the piece. But by buying it, I am supporting the artist so that she can continue

Collecting is such a personal thing. While there is a risk, if you are buying something that you truly love, you can't lose.

Sabrina Ho, Collector

creating art, which in turn inspires her artistic community to continue with this essential form of human creativity. To me, it is a way of doing good—and it comes with an object that I love and a story to tell. Today, my collection has more than eighty pieces, and it's growing. I follow a simple strategy: I buy what I like and rarely spend more than $15,000.

1.3 Strategies for Collecting

While motivations can vary broadly, strategies don't. Having interviewed many of the world's top five hundred collectors and having worked in the market for so many years, I have observed two types of collecting strategies: buying horizontally and buying vertically.

Buying horizontally, or "butterfly" buying, means purchasing from a broad range of artists—across periods, from the ancient to the contemporary, across genres, movements, mediums, and so on. In other words, it's buying what you like, with a focus emerging retrospectively. It's the most common strategy. Herbert and Dorothy Vogel are good examples, simply buying from artists whose work they liked and could afford. Buying vertically is the opposite. It means concentrating in-depth on one artist or a group of artists, often referred to as "establishing a position." Ronald Lauder's exclusively German and Austrian collection is a good example, as is Swizz Beatz and Alicia Keys's collection, which focuses on contemporary living African American artists. Komal Shah, meanwhile, devotes her collection to women artists.

Join a Kunstverein in your city and keep an eye out for Jahresgaben! Maurin Dietrich, Curator

The right strategy for you will depend on your current collecting level. If you are just starting out, you probably won't have a clear focus yet. In many of the quotes that follow, collectors will reassure you repeatedly not to worry. You will create your taste over time, and your strategy will inevitably follow. Once you have bought a few pieces and have had more exposure to the art world, your taste will become more defined and your search will narrow. Among many top collectors, I've seen a repeated correlation between collecting maturity and strategy: while an early collector tends to buy horizontally, maturity shows a move toward vertical collecting, either because they have found their focus or because they decided to work with an art advisor who narrows it for them. To reiterate, buying art demands a significant investment in time to see as much art as possible, and a collection focus only comes with time.

If you are starting to collect art, make sure you buy works that resonate with you—works that you see yourself living with and enjoy seeing every day. Follow your own instincts and do your own research—who is the artist, who owns the work, which gallery represents him.

Ronald Harrar, Collector

Another thing I learned from my many conversations with collectors: the best strategy for first-time buyers is to stay under $1,000. At this price point, you can't really go wrong. Your options are either to buy directly from artists or to buy from lower-ranked galleries. If you do want to go a bit higher, you could buy an edition of a superstar artist: an edition of a work by Damien Hirst, for example, starts at $2,000. Buying an edition is a reassuring route for many first-time buyers. You buy into a trusted brand at an affordable price, and there is at least some chance of a resale value. You can also tell your friends or your partner's mom that you have a Damien Hirst at home—most people won't even realize that it's only an edition. But primarily, it will give you a good taste of what it's like to buy art.

Buy art to collect art, not to be an "Art Collector."

Ashley Melisse Abess, Collector

The entry process is a bit like picking up a new sport. When you start playing golf, for example, you don't want to buy the best clubs, golf bag, and outfit—you just need some clubs to hit a few balls. Over time, you will get a better feeling for the sport, and you will notice the difference when hitting with different clubs. When you reach that point, you can start investing in better clubs that fit your playing style. With art, it's very similar. You need to get your feet wet before you can recognize your own style and then you can begin to invest. See a lot of art, buy at the lower end, live with your artworks for a bit, and then gradually move up and spend more.

Art is the only human commitment that can still bring hope, and we all need it. So look for hope in art—don't be driven by the market.

John Dodelande, Collector

Perhaps my most crucial tip: don't worry about making a wrong decision with your first purchase. Every collector I have ever spoken with remembers the first piece they bought. From all the works I own, my Rupprecht Geiger is still my favorite, and I remember exactly the moment I first put it on the wall. It was a great feeling and one of the reasons why I am writing this book: I want you to have this feeling too. And if you do, please share it with me! Do a story on Instagram with your first artwork—tag me, and I will reshare it.

1.4 Where to Start

So, knowing that you need to buy your first piece and shouldn't spend a lot of money on it—where do you start? Where—from the twenty thousand galleries, two thousand auction houses, unlimited online art marketplaces, thousands of artworks available at art fairs, and millions of artists with Instagram accounts—do you buy your first piece?

Filtering this exhausting choice down to a manageable size is a challenge that every art collector has faced at some point. When I asked collectors for their thoughts on where to start, they all said the same two things:

- **See as much art as you can.**
- **Talk to as many gallerists, artists, collectors, and journalists as you can.**

To give you an easy introduction, I summarize below the key institutions. We will go much deeper into each of them later on, and you will get a better understanding of where to buy and what to look out for.

Galleries

Galleries are the best resource for simply seeing art, and the best way to start going to them is to make a social event of it with friends and go to openings. They are usually on Thursdays from 6:00–8:00 p.m. Often, galleries team up and group their openings on the same day. We'll return to this later, when I will give you some tools to help you find galleries and their openings.

Gallery openings also let you widen your network. When I moved to New York, I went to four hundred galleries in a month purely to rub shoulders and get an idea of New York's local art world. From a starting point of literally no acquaintances, persistent self-introduction was leading to the beginnings of a network by the second Thursday, and gradually, I built a New York network that now includes curators, dealers, and artists. Generally, of course, buyers who are not art professionals won't be able to put in that kind of time and may live in a city with considerably fewer galleries. The point I want to make, and make early and probably repeatedly to quash any hope that there may be shortcuts, is that buying art requires dedication. It means putting the effort in and going to see it. You will need to leave your house and visit art galleries.

> **Collect what is a reflection of your time. Engage with other collectors. Buy less, choose well.**
>
> Jongsuwat Angsuvarnsiri, Collector

Once you have found a list of gallery openings in your city, you will need to go through and decide which to attend, assuming you don't have time to see all of them. In the chapter "Galleries," I talk about exactly this: how to filter galleries and categorize them so you know where to go.

Online Platforms

Among the many online art platforms to search for and purchase art, the best is probably on your phone. Instagram is by far the best resource to find art. Use Instagram and follow the galleries and artists you like. Scroll through their profiles and see what they are showing. A good starting point is to follow the accounts of galleries in your city. The often-detested social-media algorithm is your friend here: it will recommend further galleries or artists. Once you have found something you like, DM the gallery via Instagram to ask about the price. Gallerists and artists get these requests all the time, and they expect them, so don't be scared to do it.

Over the last ten years, several online platforms for buying art have emerged, but the two principal types are galleries and the artist. Gallery platforms partner with physical galleries and display artworks from all the associated galleries on the one platform, with obvious all-in-one-place advantages for the potential buyer. The most prominent is artsy.net; an alternative is platformart.com. Artist platforms are websites where you can buy direct from artists, circumventing galleries and thus often spending less, as artists do not need to price in a representative's commission. Again, these platforms cut down on (virtual) legwork by offering the works of several artists in one place. The biggest are saatchiart.com and singulart.com. In addition to these

Collecting is an intimate journey, as art creates emotions and memories. While we see a tendency to compare collections, my advice for collectors is to collect with passion, integrity, and patience and to support emerging artists. Emerging artists are a few decades away from becoming the classics and will keep inspiring new generations.

Catherine & Mamadou-Abou Sarr, Collectors

two dominant categories, a third has emerged in investment platforms. This fairly new development offers the opportunity to take shares in an artwork—rather than a physical acquisition—and thus profit from any increase in value. The main outlet so far is masterworks.com.

Artists

While some artists put their work up on artist platforms, many don't. As a result, the best way to connect with them is via Instagram. I cannot emphasize this strongly enough: start following the accounts of the artists you see and like. This has two benefits. First, a lot of artists will share invites to their shows on Instagram. They will also post updates on their work and progress in their stories, which is all part of beginning to inhabit the art world you are entering, albeit in a different role. I personally connect with artists through Instagram almost daily to keep myself informed about shows I should attend. The second benefit is that the Instagram algorithm will suggest other artists and accounts you should follow.

> **Talk to artists. Learn about their work. Fall in love and buy their art. Repeat.**
> Ryan Stanier, Art Fair Founder

I have devoted an entire chapter to artists in this book, which will help you to identify artists you should follow and buy. Don't be deterred by distance either—even if an artist is in a different city or country, art shipping has become much easier. I frequently buy from other continents via Instagram and have artworks shipped to me.

Collectors, Advisors, and Curators

If your Instagram initially seems to offer frustratingly little art, the balance will shift just a few days after you start to follow collectors, advisors, and curators. Your best starting point is to follow a company that I cofounded, @larrys_list, straightaway. Every day our team posts photos of collectors' homes, showing you how other collectors live and what art they are buying. I use this for inspiration (and must admit that I also like to see other people's decor, right down to the wall color and carpets). Following other collectors, advisors, and curators helps me to narrow down my search for new artists because I can see what other people are looking at and what they collect. Striking out in an original direction purely because it is original is not a strategy I would advise at this point: unless you have a real passion for a particular artist, take your lead from experienced collectors.

Don't collect with your ears. Collecting art should be about reflecting on how you could be an incredible steward of artworks that evoke ideas and points of view that have the capacity to change the way you think, see, and move in the world. Collect with intention, passion, and generosity.

Larry Ossei-Mensah, Curator

And for those who are really into hunting down the next superstar artists, a recent study, which Larry's List coauthored, showed that "likes" of certain collectors are solid indicators of future success for the artists. So if you are an aspiring investor collector, it is doubly important to follow collectors' accounts to see what they are looking at. We will discuss collectors in a dedicated chapter in this book. I would also recommend following those collectors who are quoted in the pages of this book.

Art Fairs

Going to galleries can be draining, particularly in a large city. Art fairs, on the other hand, are the shopping malls of the art world. You find hundreds of galleries from around the world grouped under one roof. More than three hundred art fairs take place every year, and one will be close to where you are. I recommend that every starting collector go to art fairs as early as possible. It's the easiest way for you to see a lot of art in a short time. In the chapter "Art Fairs," we will discuss how to differentiate them and how to get the best out of them once you are there.

Auction Houses

In the past, only experienced buyers bought at auction, but they now attract a much more mainstream market. Auction houses have done a good job of opening the art trade to a wider audience. Auction launches are not unlike gallery openings in their party presentation. So don't hesitate to go, even if you are not buying or only have a small budget. Auction houses may have—and to some extent have fostered—an exclusive and high-end reputation, but in reality more than 90% of all artworks sold at auction go for less than $10,000. A lot of auctions also focus on the low-end segment of the market. The terminology and mechanisms of auction houses, with things that you should be aware of, are all discussed in the "Auction Houses" chapter.

Collectors' Clubs

From all the different options above, for me, the best way to find new art is always through other collectors. Larry's List is invaluable here, but I also make good use of collectors' clubs. Wherever I lived, I have joined one of these circles that brings together new and experienced collectors and people interested in art: New York's Guggenheim Young Collectors Council, the Freunde der Nationalgalerie in Berlin, the Tate Modern membership in London, and so many more. Start looking for collector groups in your city. I have always been surprised by the quality and effort the hosts put in, and, with a yearly membership usually costing less than $1,000, it's affordable.

Don't build a collection that looks like an auction house catalogue. Buy something that is uniquely you, and tell your story.
Alan Lau, Collector

The real value of these groups is the monthly events, during which you might have the opportunity to hear a museum curator, for example, sharing their insights into the market, a new perspective on an artist you may not have really appreciated before, or an understanding of trends—you cannot put a price on hearing this kind of expertise firsthand. Private collector visits or artist studio visits are also great for new buyers. And of course, networking with other collectors in the group

Don't buy anything for a year; just go to museums, galleries, and auctions and build a library.
Philippe Ségalot, Collector

will at some point pay dividends. You don't need to be a collector to join a group—they are open to everyone. And my pro tip here would be: always look for a collector group that is affiliated with a museum. They usually have the best access to artists and to an international network.

Now that we've had this swift tour through the virtual and physical locations for seeing art, I'm now going to return to what I said initially. There are two things you need to do: see art and talk to as many people as possible. The art world is all about networking, but it's also all about the love that people have for art. People love telling their stories. They love to share excitement about a piece of art, and they love to invite you to their events, talk about their collections, and so on. Once you start building a network, invitations to events and private homes will follow.

Art has to be beautiful. So focus your collection by knowing your market. Michael Shvo, Collector

To get you started, follow these accounts on Instagram now:

- **@larrys_list**
  (see into collectors' homes for artist inspiration)
- **@artnet**
  (international art news and art-world gossip)
- **@artsy**
  (what shows are on and where)
- **@artforum**
  (one of the most established art magazines in the world)
- **@magnusresch**
  (every now and then I do free live interviews via Instagram with inspiring artists, collectors, or gallerists)

And if you like, post a photo with my book on your Instagram and tag me. I always love to hear from my readers and will make sure to reshare your post with my followers too.

Case Study

VICTORIA ROGERS—A YOUNG COLLECTOR WITH A MISSION

Victoria Rogers is a young art collector from New York City and a great example of someone whose initial interest in art and collecting sparked a philanthropic idea and, ultimately, an active way to pursue it. I spoke with her early in 2023 about her passion for promoting artists of the African diaspora and particularly women artists. "I am excited about the field's continued reckoning with racial and economic inequality. I know that for many, this work has long been a priority, but I feel as though our collective conscience has shifted, which makes me hopeful. I'm excited to be a part of a more excellent art world, deliberate in challenging systems of oppression."

Now in her early thirties, Rogers showed her determination to create change early. Not only did she earn an MBA from Stanford and an MFA from Parsons, but she also became one of the youngest trustees of a major American museum when, aged twenty-seven, she joined the board of trustees of the Brooklyn Museum and Creative Time.

Throwing the energy of her beliefs into action, in 2020 Rogers launched the Black Trustee Alliance for Art Museums, where she serves as co-chairwoman. Its mission is to transform art museums into more equitable spaces of cultural engagement by harnessing the power of Black trustees. "Arts institutions that more accurately reflect the country and their communities' demographics will fundamentally elevate the quality of those museums, increase community engagement, and, ultimately, strengthen these institutions for the future. I believe institutions are recognizing the need for change. Now is the time for transformation and a chance for the next generation to shape the future of what a cultural institution can be and stand for."

The origins of her mission are clearly visible throughout her own collection, which comprises solely African American and mostly women artists. Her energy for her ideals, though, can be traced back to her direct relationships with the artists whose work she collects and her efforts to get their works into museums through her institutional connections and her network of contacts.

Victoria is a great example of the responsible buying that I discussed above, a next-generation collector whose own passion is allied to the clear and active objective of bringing change to the inequality in the art market.

ADVICE

Art both reflects our time and shows us possibilities for what the future could be. Think about the artists you support. Do they envision a more equitable and inclusive future for everyone?

2
Investing in Art

—Why Most Art Is Not a Good Investment

"Collecting art" is used almost synonymously today with "investing in art." In anything other than specialist art publications, any news coverage of art is usually limited to the canvas bought for $1,000 that subsequently sells for $60 million. The idea of buying low and selling high is centuries old and still draws thousands of people into the art world—including the ultrarich, who, while they may have limited interest in art itself, listen attentively to bankers pushing art as a means of diversifying their portfolios.

2.1 What to Invest In

Picking wise investments is probably one of the reasons you bought this book. As I showed before, one of the top four reasons for buying art is as an investment. This is often triggered by the idea that the art market is huge. Newspapers frequently quote the art market's size as $60 billion and assert that it outperforms the stock market, using graphics like the one below to illustrate their argument. What becomes apparent is that the art market, with an increase of 8.3% per year, significantly outperforms other asset classes. This graph plots it against the S&P 500 equity index.

> **Don't think of the work as simple decoration. Buy something that draws you in—something you could stare at for a long time and see something new in it and yourself each time you gaze at it.**
>
> Kat Cohen, Collector

ART MARKET INDEX VS. S&P 500 INDEX

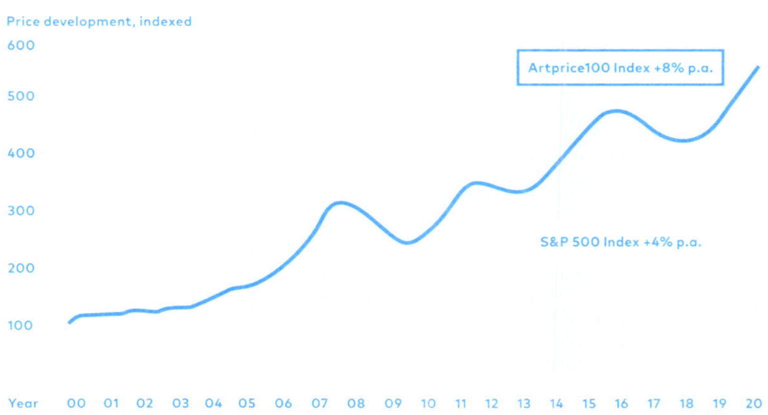

SOURCE: ARTPRICE.COM

"Before and after" comparisons are both widespread and striking, showing astonishing returns on a relatively cheap investment in only a few years. The deals in the illustration below are taken from a marketing campaign produced by an art fund. The works by Hockney, Picasso, and Basquiat show incredible returns—often up to 500% or more.

RECORD DEALS

	BOUGHT	SOLD	ABSOLUTE RETURN	IRR
HOCKNEY *The Splash* (1966)	2006	2020	+ 555.3%	+ 14.7% p.a.
PICASSO *Femme au Chien* (1962)	2012	2019	+ 455,7%	+ 28.2% p.a.
BASQUIAT *Pyro* (1984)	1996	2019	+ 3,708.4%	+ 17.2% p.a.
ZAO WOU-KI *Voie Lactée* (1966)	1998	2019	+ 3,445.9%	+ 18.5% p.a.
WU GUANZHONG *Scenery of Northern China* (1973)	2007	2020	+ 435.2%	+ 13.8% p.a.

SOURCE: ARTPRICE.COM

I have witnessed many such pitches by gallerists, dealers, auction houses, or art funds, such as masterworks.com. The art media and wider press, too, tend to lend anecdotal weight to this selective interpretation of the economic possibilities of the art market, with their obsessive "record prices" narrative. So as a potential new investor, what should you invest in to get returns that leave the S&P trailing in your wake? How can you diversify your portfolio, preferably by finding the next Basquiat? Unsurprisingly, seductive art-market figures such as those presented above tend not to reflect the underlying reality.

Heed the carpenter's advice: measure twice, cut once. In art, that translates to see, see (and see again), then buy.
Glen Bjørnholt, Collector

Financial reasons drew me to a professional role in the art market: I needed to fund my studies and decided to start selling art. As a young gallerist of only twenty, I soon realized that the booming art market so often discussed in the news was not quite what it appeared to be. Selling art was really hard, and, far from the fortune that other gallerists were allegedly making, my gallery was barely breaking even. This disparity between image and reality formed the starting point of my investigation of economics in the art market, and encouraged me to write my PhD, several books (including this one), and my research papers, and eventually to move into teaching. I wanted to understand why the media was portraying a glamorous picture of an industry that I, as a real-life practitioner, didn't experience, didn't recognize, and certainly couldn't find reflected in my bank account.

The best way to collect is to start. This means get out and see art at galleries, museums, and fairs. Research works and be confident in your eye. Know that your taste and vision may evolve; nevertheless, you have to start somewhere.

Anne Huntington Sharma, Collector

So let's take a closer look at the first graphic in this chapter again. Its message is very clear: the art index outperforms the stock market. The essential observation, however, and perhaps one not so apparent to outsiders, is that the index shows only the top one hundred performing artists: the best-selling, most traded, and most hyped names. The data for this art index reads like the who's who of the art world or the collection of the Museum of Modern Art (MoMA). Picasso, Monet, Chagall, Miró, Warhol, Magritte, Rauschenberg: every name that even school kids will recognize is included. Of course, the value of these artists never fails to rise. Even allowing for the fact that indexes are always selective, this is particularly unrepresentative for the overall market as it cherry-picks works of undisputed and pretty much irreversible value. The "sample selection bias" here, as researchers would call it, creates a decidedly misleading picture.

Don't buy anything.

Bonnie Clearwater, Museum Director

In an extensive study, my colleagues Arthur Korteweg, Roman Kräussl, and Patrick Verwijmeren exposed this flaw by creating an index that represented the art market as a whole. They looked at *all* paintings from *all* artists that were sold at auction, not only at the top artists who were traded repeatedly. Finally, they arrived at a data set of 2.3 million paintings that were traded at auction between 1960 and 2010—a far more representative picture of the art industry. They concluded that, far from outperforming the stock index, their more realistic art index fell significantly short of the S&P 500. If you isolate a tiny selection at the very top end of the market—where supply is limited and entry prices are high—you will see modest returns. But for all of the other works, returns simply don't exist, either because they don't get resold or because they are sold at a loss.

Let your instinct guide you. Buy what resonates with you, and look at your collection to find the common thread that guided you over the years. The art you buy tells you who you really are.
G. Andrea Danese, Advisor

And it doesn't stop here. Even this more balanced index, and all the others you come across (for example, the often quoted Mei & Moses index), only look at artworks that made it into auction for resale after the first purchase from a gallery or online platform. However, only a small fraction of the work that you see in galleries, art fairs, or online platforms ever get that far. Auctions, or the so-called secondary market, sell only artworks that are in demand. The reality is that less than 1% of what you see today in galleries or online platforms will ever be offered at an auction house. Either they didn't sell in the galleries in the first place and are then returned to the artist, or there is no demand to resell after their initial purchase.

Get mentors from the major auction houses to teach and guide you about the trade, starting from the ground up.
Sean, Lauren, and David Aaron Carpenter, Collectors

All of this illustrates how selection bias is employed to dramatic effect in the art market. All the marketing brochures and extravagant stock-market graphs represent only a tiny sample of all the art for sale. While it's true that this very small sample outperforms the stock market, all other works (which represent 99.9% of the artworks that are available) don't.

Of course, you can argue that stock indexes also show only a selection of companies. We all know that only a handful of companies are ever listed onthe stock exchange, mostly those with an existing track record and showing substantial outperformance over their competitors. This is as much a picture of "business" as the Artprice 100 index is a picture of "the art market," and it probably shows a similar ratio of companies founded to companies listed on the stock exchange, though most industries lack the potential for dizzying price outliers that are almost unique to the art world. As an aspiring art collector, however, the broader ratio needs to be at the forefront of your thinking. Whenever you see an artwork, you should know that art is not a good investment unless you go for the very top end of the market. And even at the top end (meaning those works that made it into an auction), only a few show a high resale value.

Buy art that punches you in the gut, makes your brain hurt, or breaks your heart. The rest is just decorating.

Dan Sallick, Collector

Collect art not for its market/resale value or because it's "trendy" but because you have developed a connection to the artist or the work.

William S. Floyd, Collector

I'm going to go on to illustrate this introduction to the business side of the art market with a brief comparison of the financial and art markets.

Liquidity

Financial markets are liquid; the art market is not. With the exception of a vanishingly small number of pieces, the work you buy today loses all resale value the moment you leave the gallery. And if you are lucky enough to have bought from an artist who actually has a resale value, be prepared to wait. Ownership changes at a much lower frequency than with stocks, and the time lag between the decision to sell and actual execution can be several months, sometimes years. In financial markets, by contrast, trading can happen immediately.

Supply and Demand

Art and artists exist in splendid oversupply, as the demand side is too small. The largest art museum in the world is made up of artists' storage spaces. And because artists don't want to pay for storage fees, it's not uncommon to burn or reuse their unsold works. While supply on the whole exceeds demand, the opposite is true, of course, at the very top end of the market. Here, there is only a limited number of artworks per artist. And when the artist dies, the supply becomes scarce. You then rely on gatekeepers to give you access that is almost entirely regulated through personal connections. If the dealer knows you, you have much better access than a person with the same capital resources who doesn't know the dealer. Access in the financial market, however, is the same for everyone who has the funds.

Collect work that is aesthetically pleasing to your eyes and feeds your brain. Phyllis Hollis, Collector

Transparency

Financial markets are more or less transparent, but the art market is characterized in part by its opacity. In the art world, insider trading is considered normal and a key source of profit. And social relationships heavily influence the price of a work. A newcomer will pay a higher price for a piece than someone else who has been buying with the gallery for many years. When you buy a stock, however, everyone gets the same price, independent of their relationship with the broker. Past transactions and owners alike are visible.

Regulations

Financial markets are highly regulated, a condition of doing business almost unknown in the art world. Cornering the market, artificially inflating prices, and insider trading are just a few practices common in the art market but forbidden in the financial sector. Consequently, while every step in the financial industry is documented in writing, almost no contracts exist in the art world. Even relationships between gallerists and artists are often based solely on handshakes, which can lead to legal disputes.

2.2 What Makes an Artwork Valuable

Continuing the analogy to the financial industries, the level of a stock price depends on a few factors, some more obvious than others. For example, when a company reports impressive profits, stock prices usually go up, and vice versa. In the art world, such objective criteria don't exist. Why do some artworks cost $10 million while others—identical, as far as one can tell—cost only $100? In the previous chapter, I spoke about art as an investment. I explained that only a small number of artists are worth investing in, as they are the only ones who show a reasonable return and are "successful" artists. So the question naturally arises: What makes an artwork valuable? But a better question, of course, is: What makes an artist valuable?

Don't stress, see as much as you can, and buy works that you gravitate toward—the ones that you still think about days later. Trust your taste, and if you don't have any, ask someone who does and trust them!

Curtis Clarizio, Collector

Measuring the success of an artist is an endlessly contentious debate. In sports, while there is always some disagreement on the criteria, supremacy can be claimed against undeniable facts: a successful runner is the fastest; the best tennis player wins the most matches; the best soccer team scores more goals. But in art, it is impossible to agree on a measure for "the best."

There is no better place to experience this paradox than in a museum gallery. You have almost certainly stood in front of an exhibit and thought: "I could do this" or "My children could do this." And you will have wondered why this seemingly easy-to-accomplish artwork is on display. The art world has a number of stock answers to this question, depending on whom you ask. If you were to ask the curator, they would likely give you a long explanation about why they chose to include the artist, citing the artist's relevance in the art world and referring to the "context" of their work in the exhibition. If you ask an art dealer the same question, they will tell you that the artist has experienced huge financial success in the market and name-drop some collectors of their work or list shows in which they have taken part. Ask a collector who admires the artist why the work is being displayed, and they will probably tell you why they find it personally inspiring. All of these answers depend on a different model of success.

Don't be afraid to lose money and buy bad art. It's a pastime that requires making mistakes to learn. Just like everything else you do in life.
Stefan Simchowitz, Gallerist

Take, for example, these two artworks: Richard Prince's *Untitled (Cowboy)* from 1999 and Norm Clasen's *Mission Ridge, Perma, MT* from 1988. If you have a laptop nearby, Google them quickly. You will notice no difference. But what if I told you that one of these artworks was valued at a few thousand dollars and the other was worth $2.5 million? Take another look: Would you be able to tell me which one was worth millions? Probably not, since one is a modification of the other. Your first instinct might be to guess that the older piece, *Mission Ridge, Perma, MT* by Clasen, has a higher value since it is the original image. You would, however, be wrong. Prince's *Untitled (Cowboy)*, based on a photocopy of the original, is worth millions, while the original by Clasen is valued at only $15,000. How is this possible?

I built my collection by listening to artists whom I admired regarding artists they admired. I have never bought a work of art that I did not love, and investment has never had anything to do with my acquisitions. Donna Rosen, Collector

2.3 Quantifying Reputation and Success in Art: A Study

Fascinated by the fact that two almost-identical works could have such wildly different values, I began to investigate the factors at play in making an artwork valuable and an artist financially successful. I reached out to Harvard data scientist Samuel Fraiberger and László Barabási, a leader in the field of network science. Over the course of three years, we analyzed the careers of 500,000 artists and looked at more than 10 million data points to try and spot the commonalities between successful artists. Artfacts.net, a leading data company in the art world, provided the data; Magnus.net provided the prices. Our paper, titled "Quantifying Reputation and Success in Art," marked a breakthrough in art-market research, and the results were published in more than a hundred newspapers around the world, including the *Economist*, the *Wall Street Journal*, the *Financial Times*, and many more.

Look, look, look, and ask questions. Don't be intimidated! And get involved with a museum.
Beth Rudin DeWoody, Collector

What we discovered was that by plotting the career effect of a powerful network of art institutions, we had created a highly informative and data-rich map. At its simplest, the map charts how art moves around the world and how institutions are linked by the artists they exhibit. Each dot represents an art institution, and the size of the dot describes the impact of the institution on the price of an artist's work. To create this, we used a mathematical concept called centrality, which is drawn from network science and which is at the core of the Google-search ranking algorithm. The proximity of the dots indicates which institutions are linked to each other and exhibit the same artists.

One hub immediately stands out, top left. My own name for this collective powerhouse, the majority of which is in

New York City, is the Holy Land. Within the Holy Land boundary is a handful of museums—MoMA, the Guggenheim, the Metropolitan Museum of Art, the Whitney Museum of American Art, and the Art Institute of Chicago. They are surrounded by a few commercial galleries—Gagosian, Pace, Hauser & Wirth, and David Zwirner. These museums and galleries are crucial because an exhibition at any of them essentially guarantees that the artist will ascend to fame and earn headline prices. The Holy Land is the definition of artistic validation.

Look at ten thousand objects before you acquire the first one. Why? Because your taste evolves so quickly in the early years of collecting. By looking at a lot of works, you are able to skip many of the early phases where your eye is not developed.

Dennis Scholl, Collector

Outside of the Holy Land, we ended up with individual clusters of small dots, which I call island networks. Island networks are all the little separate institutions that show art but that do not create truly successful artists. They are simply too small and insignificant to influence an artist's career. A convincing 99% of all institutions sit somewhere within an island network, and they will never make a real impact at the higher end of the market or change the lives of the artists represented by them.

The map shows that there is only one route to success. If an artist is not a part of the Holy Land, then they are stuck inan island network, with all its limitations. There, the probability is low that they will ever cross thebridge to the Holy Land and become a big name in the art world. The majority of artists who start in an island-network institution never surpass this level, whereas artists who begin exhibiting in Holy Land institutions tend to stay at the top.

Train your eye first by visiting museums, galleries, auctions, and looking at art books. Your newly acquired expertise will delight you.

Walda Besthoff, Collector

To expand on this, we were able to see that the first five to ten exhibitions are the most critical for artists; after that, the trajectory, statistically speaking, becomes very predictable. If an artist is picked up by a top gallery early on, the chances of becoming established among the elite are excellent. If, however, an invitation to show at any of the high-ranked institutions doesn't arrive within the first five shows, then it is unlikely ever to come. There have been very few rags-to-riches stories. In fact, no more than 240 artists (0.048% of the sample we analyzed) who began exhibiting at low-prestige institutions ever made it to the top.

DISTRIBUTION OF INSTITUTIONS AND THEIR IMPORTANCE

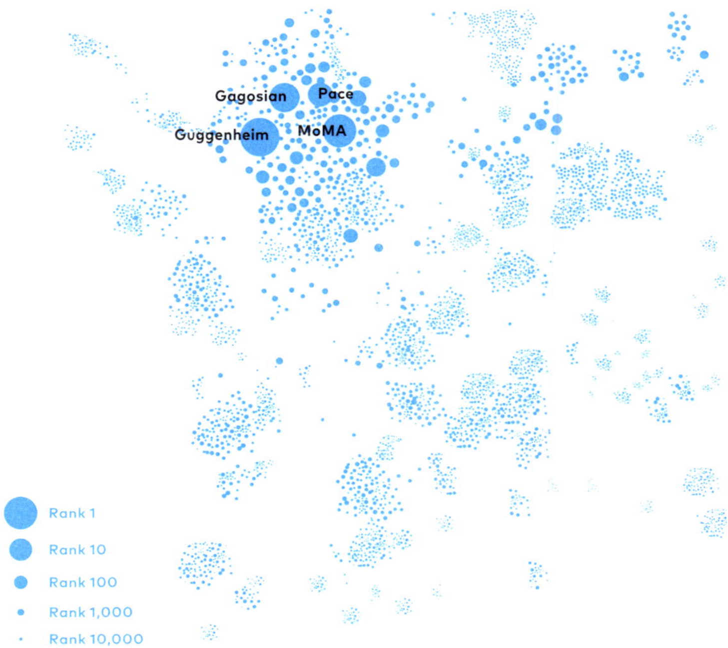

FRAIBERGER, SINATRA, RESCH, RIEDL, BARABÁSI (2018)

2.4 Implications for Collectors

Coming back to the original question of why Richard Prince's copy of Norm Clasen's work sells for so much more, the answer lies in the network. Prince is deeply rooted in the Holy Land: he is represented by Gagosian and has had shows at the MoMA, the Guggenheim, and the Met. Clasen, in contrast, shows with little-known galleries that are a part of island networks. In an interview with Artsy in 2018, he said, "If you see somebody's copied your work, there's something deep down in you that says, 'I'm the author of that. Somebody took that work and rephotographed it. They're not the ones that were out there lying with the rattlesnakes, the ants, the mosquitos.'" His frustration is understandable. And I am sure many artists often feel the same way when they look at works in museums. Since you, as a collector, now understand the importance of gallery representation that underlies this, you can use it to your advantage if you hope to collect resalable art.

Educate yourself before you take the plunge, go to the art fairs, the museums, and the galleries. Define your taste, and only buy what you love.
Michael Cohen, Collector

Creating a collection is mainly the art of compromise. This means thinking of the collection as a whole, as a work of art in itself.
Michał Borowik, Collector

When I presented this study to my aspiring collector friends, they all asked me the same questions: How do I find the artists in the Holy Land? When quality is so subjective, how do I know that I am not buying total rubbish and that I am not getting ripped off? This book will provide the tools to help you navigate the art market to help you find answers.

Before we jump into this, here are some implications a collector can draw from my study:

(1) Most art is not a good investment
Only a few artists make it to stardom and serve as an investment. Almost all other artists and galleries are stuck in island networks and will not see an increase in prices. Understanding this at the start of your collecting journey is important. If you are purely interested in making money, you will have to focus exclusively on artists and galleries that form the population of the Holy Land. However, if you are interested in collecting art for any other motive (and consider it a cherry on top if the art increases in value), then the whole art market can be your hunting ground. In the next chapters, I explain how you can differentiate between artists so you always know if the artist you are considering has investment potential or not.

Buy art you love and want to live with. Anna Weyant, Artist

(2) Networking is key
The art world is a people business: in the absence of objective criteria for good art, the network takes over. That's why networking is so relevant—for artists but also for collectors. As a collector you need to observe these networks and tap into them. Talk to people, talk to artists, and go to openings. Get a feeling for the scene. In this book I present the key stakeholders that drive the strength of my theoretical Holy Land. Networking with them will allow you to understand what they are looking at.

(3) Location matters
New York is the center of the art world. It's there where the most important collectors, museums, and galleries are. If you are in Berlin or Hong Kong, of course you must engage with your local art scene, but always keep in mind that superstar artists are made in New York. So if you are really looking for the next Basquiat, focus your attention there.

(4) Forget about the terms "good art" and "bad art"
For our purposes, the terms "good art" and "bad art" are irrelevant. Good art is decided by a few influencers in the Holy Land based on subjective criteria. "Bad art" is everything else. I suggest we reject these terms. Everything can

be good or bad art. It's all about the positioning, and it's highly subjective, so don't listen to anyone when buying art. Whatever you like is good art.

2.5 An Investment Strategy for Every Budget

The reality of my research often leaves my collector friends a little crestfallen. Generally, they understand that art is not a good investment and will not increase in value unless they buy from the very expensive top galleries. So they always want to know: What should we do with our modest budget of $1,000 to $50,000?

Trust your art dealer.
Marc Glimcher, Gallerist

To answer this question, I developed two frameworks—the Artist Framework (below) and the Budget Framework, which appears in a later chapter. They help you to:

- **Analyze immediately the investment potential of any artist.**
- **Classify each gallery to understand if they are in the Holy Land.**
- **Understand prices and evaluate them so you don't get ripped off.**
- **Select the right art fair for you.**
- **Select an auction house to buy/sell from.**
- **Help you decide if you need an art advisor and how to select one.**

Throughout the book, we will come back to each of these key terms. While it might be baffling now, don't worry. After reading this book, these frameworks will be clear and will become lasting dependable tools for your investing life.

2·5·1
Artist Framework

The Artist Framework shows all the key players of the art world: artists, galleries, art fairs, auction houses, and advisors. Each player is divided into several classifications. In an industry that is crowded with millions of artists and thousands of galleries, these help you to differentiate among them.

ARTIST FRAMEWORK

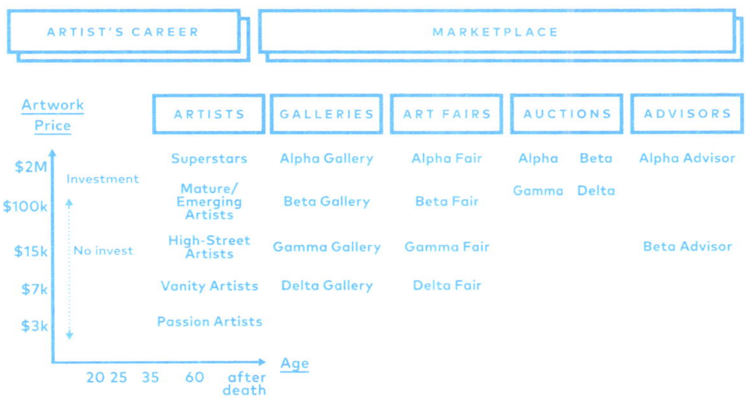

The framework can be broken up into two big columns: artists to the left; marketplaces where artists are traded to the right (galleries, art fairs, auction houses, and advisors). Artists are on the left because any activity in the art world starts with them. The categories I introduce are superstar, mature, and emerging artists, and high-street, vanity, and passion artists. In a later chapter I will explain each role in detail and what is distinctive about them, but to give you an idea at this point,

Art should not be seen as an investment, so don't look at it as a currency or a stock—trade from the emotion and understanding of the artwork.
Torsten Butzen, Collector

superstar artists, as the name suggests, are the leading fifty artists in the world. They are all household names, such as Picasso, Monet, and Warhol, and living artists such as Jeff Koons and Damien Hirst.

Galleries are the first trading platform among marketplaces. So they follow to the right, divided into alpha, beta, gamma, and delta galleries. I did the same for other platforms where art is sold: art fairs, auction houses, and advisors.

Don't read books on how to collect art. Read books on art, artists, and art history. Knowledge inspires. You will also discover how greatly collectors in the past contributed to the development of artistic careers. Marta Gnyp, Gallerist

The vertical axis is labeled with average price points rather than ranges. So for example, if an original piece costs $7,000, the artist is likely to be a vanity artist. If prices are more in the range of millions of dollars, you would expect the artist to be a superstar. I have also added investment potential for each artist. As you can see, only superstar artists and some mature/emerging artists have investment potential.

The x-axis shows a time frame that represents the artist's lifetime. In my research study, we found out that very early on in an artist's career, it's decided if the artist becomes a superstar or a vanity artist. After five to ten exhibitions, or at the age of around thirty-five, career levels are likely to be fixed. The gallery level thus starts at the age of thirty-five and doesn't change: artists will remain at their level for the rest of their lifetime and beyond.

Invest in the work and career of artists who can impact the future of our society.
Delphine Diallo, Artist

When you apply this framework as a collector, you immediately know that when you walk into an alpha gallery (and there are only four alpha galleries, but I discuss how to classify galleries more broadly in a later chapter), the gallery will be showing alpha artists. You also know which fairs the gallery is showing at and have a rough idea of average price points.

Additionally, when you look at the works of a superstar artist, you instantly know that they are sold through alpha auction houses and offered at alpha art fairs and alpha galleries. These have investment potential, and you will almost certainly need an alpha art advisor to help you get access to them. Their prices will be in the high six-digit to multi-million-dollar range.

Follow your heart and eye. Create your own signature collection. Nicola Erni, Collector

In contrast, a vanity artist is shown in delta galleries that participate at delta art fairs. Her works are not sold in auction houses. There is no investment potential, and price points will be around $7,000 for unique large pieces.

To forestall the questions that I think you will likely have at this point, I restate my reassurance that the following chapters of this book explain exactly how you tell a beta gallery from a gamma, a high-street artist from a vanity artist, and a beta art fair from a gamma auction house. All of these questions are answered as we move through the book and discuss each key player and how to differentiate between the key players. After reading this book, you will be able to walk into a gallery and know exactly who you are dealing with or look at an artist and immediately estimate the price point.

Always go with your gut when selecting an artwork, and collect for the love of collecting rather than for any potential profit.
Sandra Neumann, Collector

These frameworks also reveal one of the advantages of the art market: while the market seems confusing from the outside, there is a surprising structure within the market. Once you understand the key concepts and have familiarized yourself with the key players, the structure should last for at least the next ten years or so. Art may be highly dynamic, but the structure that governs the market is not.

Case Study

LUCIEN SMITH—THE BIGGEST ART-MARKET INVESTMENT

The spectacular ascent and sharp corrective in Lucien Smith's early career is a cautionary tale for collectors hoping they've discovered the new Basquiat. It illustrates precisely why the wider dynamics of the art market matter and why a wise investor will make decisions based on sound evidence of exhibition history and representation rather than gamble on chatter.

Born in 1989, Smith was one of the most hyped artists of the early 2010s. In 2013 he looked unstoppable: Just two years after graduating from the Cooper Union, one of his works sold on the secondary market for nearly $400,000. He was the wunderkind of the art media, and he appeared in Forbes's "30 Under 30" two years in a row. Yet in 2015 Smith decided to step out of the market and dramatically reduced his gallery shows. Today, many of his works have either been "bought-in" (not sold) or have gone for between $5,000 and $20,000—a dizzying drop from the $400,000 his works once achieved and a fall that bruised a lot of collectors who ended up carrying a loss on their acquisitions.

I am a big admirer of Smith's work, but a lot of people got far too excited far too early. During 2014, shortly after leaving art school, Smith's work was massively played up, with investors fighting to get pieces that were selling repeatedly for more than $200,000. Within a few short months, by mid-2015, the market had cooled dramatically, and Smith's prices never reasserted themselves to their former level.

A smart investor would have realized that Smith was just at the beginning of his career and that prices over $100,000 were overinflated and highly susceptible to collapse. Smith simply had not had the museum-show exposure and did not yet have alpha-gallery representation.

Harsh though the experience of financial loss might have been for would-be investors, the emotional effect on Smith was profound. In our various interviews, Smith is clear-sighted about the negative effects of his sharp rise to fame and his eventual personal crisis and disillusionment with his artistic process. The expectations were far too high, and he feels the market left him exposed without any way to protect himself or navigate around it. Today, he has started to show works again, albeit very selectively, including a museum show in 2020 at the Parrish Art Museum in the Hamptons. Inspired by his experience, he also founded Serving the People (STP), an arts nonprofit that intends to create a multidisciplinary program free of commercial bias. Lucien's exposure to a free market, badly distorted by the rush to flip his works, was a painful one. Nonetheless, it proved the catalyst that led him to reinvent himself outside of the main-stream art market. Smith's price development is a powerful cautionary tale for everyone who thinks that it's easy to make money in the art market and a warning for all those who "buy with their ears" and rush toward the latest name without reflection and analysis. This book provides the tools to sidestep the same trap.

ADVICE

Buy what you like.

3
Navigating the Art Market

—Data, Players, Power Structures

I'm often amazed by how little most collectors know about the art market's history, power structure, and significant participants. Understanding its past, like any other market, may help forecast its future. This chapter should provide you with a broad overview of the art market and ensure that you grasp the key phrases.

3.1 History of the Art Market

3·1·1
Record Prices

Looking at record prices—and who paid them and where—can help you comprehend the history of the art market. Auction records from 1700 to the present illustrate that art has a long history of setting record values. However, outlier results have reached much more dramatic levels in recent years, and they are set in a context in which the broader top-end art market is more expensive in real terms than it was in 1700. The greatest price for an artwork in 1701 was £320; in 2017, we witnessed a record-breaking £340,000,000. Of course, three centuries of change in the value of money devalues this comparison. The crucial point for our purposes is that the biggest and fastest rises in both price anomalies and more accurately anticipated high-end art prices have occurred since 2010.

Look at a lot of art before acquiring anything and ask a lot of questions. It's a gallery's job to help educate their clients, and people shouldn't be afraid.
Karen Boyer, Advisor

Record prices also show us how buyers have changed. Public institutions no longer play a relevant role: the last time a public institution paid a record price was 1985, when the Getty Museum bought Mantegna's *Adoration of the Magi* (ca. 1495–1505). Individual buyers known as ultra-high-net-worth individuals, or UHNWI, mostly men, mostly with a finance background, and until recently mostly American, have taken over since. This might change, though. The current record holder came out of the Middle East, when Saudi Arabia's minister of culture, Prince

Only buy what really speaks to you—what you truly love.
Steven Guttman, Collector

Badr bin Abdullah bin Mohammed bin Farhan Al Saud, paid £340 million ($450,312,500) for da Vinci's *Salvator Mundi* (ca. 1500).

And the geographical center for high-value sales shifted too: from eighteenth-century Amsterdam to nineteenth-century Paris and London before settling in New York—specifically, the New York branches of Sotheby's and Christie's. Going ahead, this dynamic history suggests that the center might shift away from New York at any point to a new principal location.

The success of an artist is about the work. It doesn't have anything to do with the market.
Julian Schnabel, Artist

Another notable feature of this list of record-breaking prices is that all artworks are paintings, from Europe, and produced by males. This bias toward European male painters is currently encountering significant problems in the modern market, but it has been sufficiently internalized over time to give a long-term advantage to white male artists, strengthening reasonable claims of a lack of democracy across the market.

RECORD-BREAKING SALE PRICES FOR PAINTINGS

YEAR	GBP	ARTIST	AUCTIONER & LOCATION	BUYER
1701	320	Dou	Amsterdam	(Unknown)
1811	5,250	Rembrandt	Christie's, London	Prince Regent George IV
1910	28,250	Hals	Amer. Art Assoc., New York	Henry C. Frick
1970	2,310,000	Velázquez	Christie's, London	Metropolitan Museum
1985	8,100,000	Mantegna	Christie's, London	J. Paul Getty Museum
2010	65,001,250 70,452,891	Giacometti Picasso	Sotheby's, London Christie's, New York	Lily Safra (Unknown)
2012	74,003,394	Munch	Sotheby's, New York	Leon Black
2013	89,411,063	Bacon	Christie's, New York	Elaine Wynn
2015	102,600,00	Picasso	Christie's, New York	(Unknown)
2017	340,000,00	da Vinci	Christie's, New York	Prince Bader

SOURCE: SPAENJERS, GOETZMANN, MAMONOVA (2014)

3.2 The Art Market Today

3·2·1 Fine Art Categories

It's common for my friends to say they like modern art when I ask about their art preferences. However, when I inquire about specific artists, they typically mention contemporary ones such as Dash Snow or Marilyn Minter. In reality, they are referring to contemporary art rather than modern art. To clarify the definition of Fine Art, I will outline the five main categories that encompass it:

The first is **Old Masters**, which refers to artists born between 1250 and 1750, including famous names such as Albrecht Dürer, Michelangelo, and Rembrandt van Rijn.

The second category is **Nineteenth-Century Art**, spanning the years 1800 to 1900 but excluding modern art. This category includes artists such as J. M. W. Turner, Caspar David Friedrich, and Eugène Delacroix.

Modern Art is the third category, overlapping with nineteenth-century art on a timeline but comprising artists born between 1850 and 1910 who pushed the boundaries of art in new ways. Examples of modern art include Vincent van Gogh, Wassily Kandinsky, and Piet Mondrian, all of whom are frequently displayed at MoMA.

The fourth category is **Postwar Art**, which encompasses artists born between 1910 and 1944, such as Jackson Pollock, Yves Klein, and Sol LeWitt.

Finally, **Contemporary Art** covers artists born after 1945, including some of the highest-paid artists of all time, such as Jeff Koons, Damien Hirst, and Cecily Brown. It is worth noting that the boundaries between these categories can be fluid and subject to interpretation.

3·2·2

Players and Trading Levels

The art market is primarily composed of two main groups: artists and collectors. These two groups are integral to the workings of the art world, with artists supplying artwork and collectors generating demand for it. Other players in the art market, such as galleries, museums, and institutions, act as intermediaries between artists and collectors. These intermediaries can be divided into two groups: commercial art mediators and conceptual art mediators.

Art is like drinking a great whiskey: buy what you like and, most importantly, enjoy the experience. Julie Macklowe, Collector

Commercial art mediators, such as galleries, facilitate the transaction of art between artists and collectors, often acting as a reference for either side. On the other hand, conceptual art mediators transfer knowledge about art to the public, for example through museum exhibitions. While they do not engage in direct transactions like galleries, their impact on the art market can be just as powerful, if not more so. Both types of mediators play an important role in the art market, helping to sustain the exchange of art and ideas.

Buy art that is personal to you and a reflection of your own experience. That way, no matter what ups and downs or trends the art market goes through, you will always be happy with your acquisition because it means something personally significant to you.

Amitha Raman, Collector

As previously mentioned, this market can be divided into two categories: the primary market and the secondary market. The following diagram highlights these two markets, which will be discussed further.

TRADING LEVELS AND PLAYERS IN THE ART MARKET

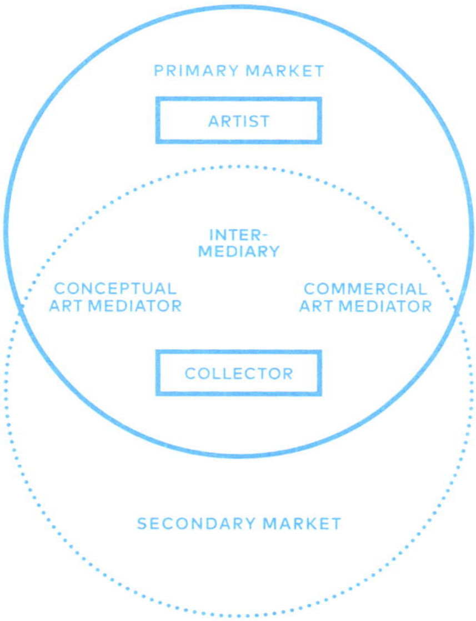

COMMERCIAL ART MEDIATOR
- Art galleries
- Private art dealers
- Auction houses
- Art fairs
- Online art platforms
- Ancillary art business providers

CONCEPTUAL ART MEDIATOR
- Museums/Kunsthalle/NP
- Media

SOURCE: RESCH, 2011

The primary market is the initial market where art is traded, primarily involving living artists and galleries. This market has a larger number of artists and buyers compared to the secondary market. Private sales are the norm, leading to opaque pricing, small margins, and low liquidity. Most practicing artists operate in this market, and the works sold here usually lack resale value.

On the other hand, the secondary market involves the trading of art for at least the second time. Auction houses are the major players in this market, alongside established galleries and dealers with substantial funds and inventories. The secondary market sees fewer artists traded, and the number of potential buyers with significant resources is also smaller.

Competition is widespread in the primary market due to a large number of artists trying to sell to a limited number of buyers. Conversely, the secondary market is different, with few artists successfully making it into the market and fewer potential buyers with significant resources. Key players in this market can exercise a great deal of influence over an artist's success and manipulate future price expectations.

3.3 Art Market Data

3·3·1 Overview

Understanding the numerical data in the art market is crucial, and as a believer in its importance, I urge collectors to have a basic understanding of art-market statistics. Unfortunately, accurate statistics are seldom found in the media, where references to "more than three hundred thousand galleries" are frequently made without precision. However, my team has conducted research by scrutinizing phone books, Google Maps, and other databases to arrive at a rough breakdown of the numbers.

> **If you are a true collector in your personality, follow your heart . . . but if you see art as a business opportunity, hire the services of an expert.** Doron Sebbag, Collector

- **40,000 museums**
- **20,000 galleries**
- **1,400 auction houses**
- **100,000 art advisors**
- **6,000 important art buyers**

(meaning they spend more than $100,000 a year on art)

VALUE AND VOLUME IN THE ART MARKET

YEAR	VALUE ($BN)	VOLUME (M)
2009	$40	31
2010	$57	35
2011	$65	37
2012	$57	36
2013	$63	37
2014	$68	39
2015	$64	38
2016	$57	36
2017	$64	39
2018	$68	40
2019	$64	41
2020	$50	31
2021	$66	37
2022	$68	38

SOURCE: ART BASEL REPORT, 2023

Around forty million artworks are bought and sold annually by the various players in the art market, which suggests that the market's value is estimated between $55 billion and $70 billion as of 2023. However, different reports have quoted widely varying numbers, making it difficult to determine the exact size of the market. It is noteworthy that FedEx's revenue in 2022 was $93 billion, which means that a single player in the transportation market generates more revenue than all the galleries, auction houses, dealers, advisors, and online platforms in the art market combined. Despite the seemingly large figures, the art market is relatively small. Moreover, the market has not shown much growth in the past decade, as the revenue figure of $65 billion remains stable. To summarize a point that should by this time be very clear: all the chatter about a booming art

Identify an especially compelling theme to help guide you through the vast range of works.

Dorothée Wahl, Collector

Don't purchase art just for the sake of financial gain—develop deep knowledge and collect out of passion.

Benedict Rodenstock, Collector

market is largely exaggerated. Only the top end is booming. The rest is really not in good shape.

3·3·2
What Sells Where

When we examine the art market by value, the data from the secondary market provides a more realistic perspective. Despite accounting for only 1% of the lots, works that sold for more than a million dollars make up 60% of the market's value. On the other hand, seven in ten artworks sell for less than $5,000, representing only 2% of the market's value. This disparity highlights the domination of a few artists and the extreme inequality in the distribution of money and power in the market. The market is also geographically concentrated, with the US, UK, and China accounting for 80% of sales, while countries such as Germany, France, and Italy play a negligible role. These findings challenge the common perception of the art market as a space where vast amounts of money are distributed equitably.

Identify a point of focus—medium, subject matter, type of artist, or something as simple as a color—and stick to it. With so many fairs and galleries to visit, it will help make decisions and build a real collection.
Marlies Verhoeven Reijtenbagh, Collector

DISTRIBUTION OF SOLD ARTWORKS IN AUCTIONS ACCORDING TO PRICE LEVEL

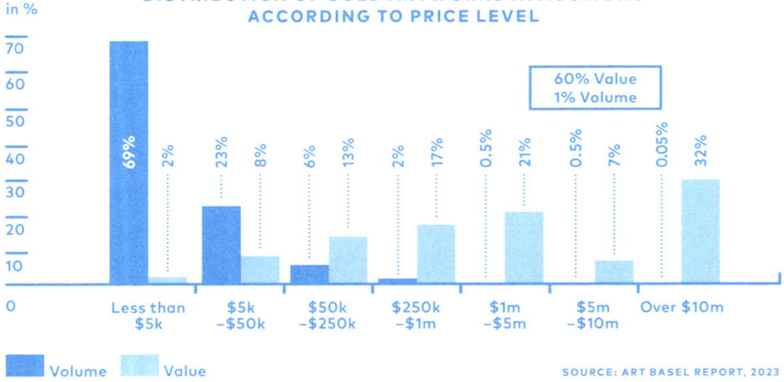

SOURCE: ART BASEL REPORT, 2023

3.4 Online Art-Market Data

In contrast to other industries, the art world has been minimally affected by the rise of online trading. Online sales represent only 16% of global sales value, which is relatively small when compared to the significant impact of the internet on other offline retailers.

However, the COVID-19 pandemic has changed this balance. In 2020 online art sales doubled from the previous year and reached their peak in 2021, with $13.3 billion in sales. Although online sales have since decreased to around $11 billion, this is still much higher than pre-pandemic levels. However, buyers in the primary market have remained loyal to offline buying, and online sales mostly occur for works priced at less than $5,000. Even in the secondary market, the average online lot value at auction houses such as Christie's is only about $8,000.

Instagram will have the same impact on the art market as YouTube had on the music industry. The online market is here to stay. Simon de Pury, Auctioneer

3.5 Female, LGBTQ+, and Artists of Color

Current research indicates that female artists, members of the LGBTQ+ community, and artists of color are facing significant underrepresentation in the art market. They are not given equal opportunities in terms of exhibitions, prices, sales, and gallery representation when compared to their white male peers. The art market is characterized by systemic inequality, where a small number of mostly white male painters dominate the industry.

Studies focused on gender inequality in the art market reveal that women, in particular, are facing the following issues. (Due to the lag in published research, discussions on gender inequality mostly refer to male and female terms.)

- **Only 33% of artists exhibited globally were women in 2018.**
- **Only 10% of galleries represent a fifty-fifty split of male and female artists.**
- **At auctions, women's artworks fetch much lower prices than men's. Only two works by women have ever broken into the top 100 auction sales for paintings.**
- **In 2018 men created 92% of all lots and 95% of the total value of art sold at auction.**
- **The number of resold works by men still far outstrips those by women. A study by Mei Moses shows 2,472 repeat sales by 499 female artists, compared to 55,706 repeat sales by 8,477 male artists in the period 2012–19.**
- **Only 11% of acquisitions and 15% of exhibitions at thirty-one key US museums between 2008 and 2020 were of work by female-identifying artists.**
- **During that same period at those thirty-one museums, acquisitions of artwork by Black American women artists amounted to half of 1%—that's a fraction of a percent.**
- **This significant gender disparity is only underscored by the fact that women form the majority of those training and working as visual artists. In main arts colleges too, statistics show that the balance leans strongly toward women, with an average 65% female-student share of enrollment in art programs in the US and UK.**

Bypass the market-makers and go directly to the studio; the relationship with the artist will result in a more personal, meaningful collection, plus save you a couple of bucks!

Katarina Feder, Art Tech Founder

Case Study

KOMAL SHAH—AN ACTIVIST FOR WOMEN-IDENTIFYING ARTISTS AND PEOPLE OF COLOR

Komal Shah is another example of an art collector driven to take positive action by the inequality in the market. Today, she is one of the largest collectors of works by women-identifying artists and people of color. "For far too long, many women have been sidelined by their male peers and excluded from the canon by restrictive gatekeepers. These are fantastic artists, full stop. Gender identity shouldn't have any effect, but we know it does affect how these artists are received, contextualized, and appreciated."

Like many collectors, Shah's professional life started far from the creative industries. Hailing from Ahmedabad, India, she studied at Stanford University, earned her MBA from Berkeley, and went on to serve in several high-profile tech roles. A shift in priorities in 2008 led her to cofound the mission-driven Shah Garg Collection, which spotlights women-identifying artists and people of color. She now sits on the board of various museums—including SFMOMA, the Hammer Museum, and the Studio Museum in Harlem—and leads the quarterly Stanford conversation series Artists on the Future for her alma mater.

Her collecting habit has undergone a clear evolution from a focus on abstract painting to a collection driven by her advocacy for those she sees as marginalized by a dominant male culture. As she has continued to grow as a collector, the breadth of the collection has expanded thematically and conceptually beyond painting to sculpture, ceramics, and textiles, with a strong interest in economically and culturally reevaluating work formerly, and derisively, described as "women's work" or "craft." Her mission has now developed into an authoritative position in this niche but vital part of a wider push to reframe traditionally sidelined artistic work.

Shah is one of many excellent examples among collectors who are driven by the aspiration of changing the narrative for underrepresented artists and, in her case, forms of art that have been both culturally and economically undervalued. She not only buys from artists of this group, but she also works to raise awareness of the topic. "It's unjust, and I hope that by continuing to champion our collection's mission, we will mobilize other collectors, curators, and museum directors to rectify and reach parity."

ADVICE

Collect what you love and believe in–it is nearly impossible to predict the market, but you will have surrounded yourself with joy and wonder. Support and learn from museum curators; they are an invaluable source of knowledge. And nothing beats sheer mileage: visit as many museums, biennials, art fairs, and galleries as you can, so that you start developing your own collecting vision.

4
Collectors

—Learning from Other Collectors

In my view, every new collector needs to understand who their peers are, as for centuries collectors have been the essential counterpart to artists themselves in the art world. While artists supply, collectors establish the market by generating demand and bringing money into the cycle. They are also absolutely fundamental to the overall success of an artist. If a collector endorses an artist's work, the artist's value can suddenly go up—considerably so, if the collector has influence.

4.1 Overview and Classification

Collectors fall into three categories: private individuals, companies, and public institutions. Of these groups, private collectors represent by far the largest and, together with public institutions, share the clearest rationale. Corporate art collections, meanwhile, are established to diversify the assets of a corporation, to cultivate the company's image, and to improve the working environment. In very much the same way as superstar artists create most of the value on the supply side of the market, a tiny fraction of collectors who account for nearly all the turnover dominate the spending on the demand side.

I have classified collectors into five categories according to their spending (in terms of volume, not value):

- **One-time buyers: 99%**
- **Art lovers: 0.25%**
- **Investors: 0.25%**
- **Dealers: 0.25%**
- **Corporate buyers: 0.25%**

COLLECTOR BREAKDOWN

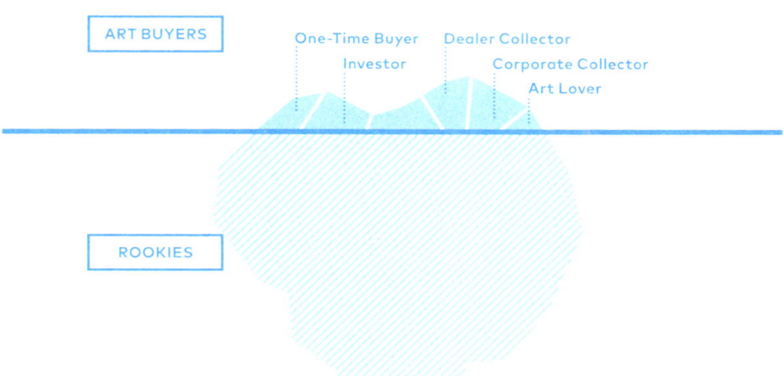

One-Time Buyers

Most people who buy art (99%) are what I call one-time buyers. In reality, such buyers might make a second or even a third purchase during their lifetime, but they will never acquire a ton of art and are decidedly buyers rather than collectors. They often want to advertise their cultural sophistication and their place in the class system, and they probably also buy as a pragmatic matter of house decor. This huge group is typically composed of buyers in their late twenties and older, usually with a good education and earning a high income. These buyers tend to acquire art from local galleries or maybe from an art fair in their city. Often, they enjoy the event more than the art, and they have little interest in the artist, whom they have never met.

Buy what you love and don't be afraid of making mistakes. It will only help to sharpen your eye and taste even more. Claus Busch Risvig, Collector

Art Lovers

Art lovers (0.25%) are old-school collectors with a true love of and fascination with art. Typically in their late fifties or older with a good education and a high income, they buy art not just to fill empty walls but also because they love it—they are inspired by it, and they find it exciting to support working artists. Those who have been well and truly colonized by the collector bug are constantly exploring to extend their collections, getting involved in the wider market, building connections with the artists themselves and with public institutions, to which they might loan artworks as part of a public-education program. After their death they will probably donate their collections to museums or other public institutions. Examples of this type of collector are Susan and Michael Hort or Rosa and Carlos de la Cruz.

Research smaller dealers, galleries, and curators who have established track records for discovering young artists who eventually have successful careers. Have them introduce you to their new discoveries and start collecting the ones you love. Troy Carter, Collector

Investors

Investors (0.25%) are buying art primarily for the return they will make on it through its eventual resale, though it is not their main profession. Slightly younger than art lovers, those among this group are mid-thirties and older, highly educated, with a high income, and with an international presence. They are regular buyers and their impact on the price and market for an artist is considerable. Some of these collectors may build their own museums to house their collections after their death. Examples of investor collectors are Steve Cohen and Daniel Loeb.

Dealer Collectors

Dealer collectors (0.25%) are demographically similar to investor collectors: mid-thirties and older, highly educated, with a high income and an international presence. They too are motivated by returns, but for dealer collectors it is their primary business. They also have a career defining influence on the eventual success of any individual artist. They have very good reputations in the art world for their wide knowledge of the market, and they maintain a network of dealers in their close circle. A dealer's collection will change in style, content, and value as their life progresses, and before their death, they will probably sell off most of it. Examples are Peter Brant, Adam Lindemann, and the Mugrabi family.

> **The twenty-first-century collector must think beyond established boundaries. The next big thing to disseminate the joy of collecting may be through collaborations between artists, designers, and brands. The best examples are the ones of Virgil Abloh with IKEA, Nike, and Vuitton. It will allow people to bring creativity and beauty into their homes and begin to create their own Wunderkammer.**
>
> Sylvain Levy, Collector

Corporate Buyers

Corporate buyers (0.25%) come from established international firms and buy to create an inspirational environment for employees, or for marketing purposes, or to put a sheen on their corporate identity. Corporate buyers will loan artworks to museums or have global exhibitions of the entire collection. Examples of these collectors are Deutsche Bank, UBS, and Würth.

Rookies

The collectors I've described above make up 100% of buyers in the market, but they are only the tip of a much larger iceberg. Thinking on a much larger scale, most of the potential in the art market lies among those who are completely new to it. They are unseen and unknown and have not bought anything . . . yet. This is in many ways the most exciting group. I call them rookies. At any regular gallery opening night, you will see a hundred people, among whom one, maybe two, are buying a piece and ninety-eight are just drinking the wine. If you eliminate those who admittedly can't afford to buy anything, this still leaves a really interesting group of twenty to thirty people who are potential customers but who need coaxing over the line to buy. I expect some of my readers to be in this group, as they represent the largest group of people frequenting the art market: those who like art but do not know what to buy.

Most contemporary art shows no return. If you buy against trends, you will do well.

Isabelle Bscher, Gallerist

4.2 Key Collectors

A few collectors have sufficient influencer power that they can manipulate the market. Via larryslist.com I have spoken to many of the most influential individuals, and you can find many of the interviews that our team did on the website. ARTnews Top 200 Collectors, which is published every year, will also give you a list of important collectors. Listed below are a handful of the most prominent collectors in the world so you can familiarize yourself with at least a few names that you will come across in your journey through the art world.

The Mugrabi Family (US)

The Mugrabi family are major dealer collectors. Jose Mugrabi was born into a Syrian Jewish family in Jerusalem before moving to Colombia at age sixteen. In 1982 he moved to New York and met Jeffrey Deitch, the uber successful art dealer and curator, who encouraged him to begin collecting. After starting his collection, Mugrabi began dealing on his own and eventually made it his primary business. The Mugrabis currently own the largest collection of Andy Warhol works (more than eight hundred pieces) and regularly bid at auction for Warhols. Jose's children, Alberto and David, are also involved in the business and will likely continue their father's work after his death.

Always buy what you love and want to live and grow with, not something you think will only be a good investment!

Roya Sachs, Curator

Bernard Arnault (France)

Bernard Arnault is the owner of the luxury brand group LVMH (Louis Vuitton Moët Hennessy) and no. 1 on *Forbes*'s World's Billionaires List 2023 with a net worth of $210 billion. He is classified as an art lover, and he both constructed the Fondation Louis Vuitton in Paris (designed by Frank Gehry) and donated approximately $219 million to rebuild Notre Dame after the fire in April 2019.

Adrian Cheng (China)

Born in 1979, Adrian Cheng is one of the world's youngest billionaires and the chairman and general manager of the real estate company New World Development in Hong Kong. He is an investor collector, with a focus on collecting contemporary Chinese art. Cheng also founded K11 Art Foundation, in their own words a "not-for-profit organization that promotes the long-term development of the contemporary art scene in Greater China."

No passion. No collecting.

Cyril Blot-Lefèvre, Collector

Mera and Don Rubell (US)

Mera and Don Rubell are true art lovers. Having collected for fifty years, they focus on collecting in-depth and supporting young artists. Their approach is to buy early in an artist's career and usually amass several pieces from each artist. The couple's massive collection of more than seven thousand works includes those by Jean-Michel Basquiat, Keith Haring, Damien Hirst, Jeff Koons, Cindy Sherman, Kara Walker, and Andy Warhol. In December 2019 the Rubells opened the Rubell Museum in Miami and followed it up in October 2022 with another outpost, at the time of writing the newest part of their collection space, in Washington, DC.

> **Only buy living artists. They need your money more than those who have passed already.**
>
> Donald Robertson, Artist

UBS Art Collection (Switzerland, headed by Mary Rozell)

The UBS Art Collection (owned by UBS Group AG) is one of the most important corporate collections in the world. It includes works by all the important artists since the 1960s, such as Basquiat, Warhol, and Gerhard Richter. Overall, the collection is home to thirty thousand pieces, which are shared with the public, either through loans to museums or in lobbies worldwide.

4.3 Collector Data

4.3.1 Art Buyers in Numbers

The total number of art buyers is hard to calculate. What we do know is that the group at the top is very few in number. My team set out to count the number of buyers who spend more than $100,000 on art annually, a figure that would almost certainly exclude one-time buyers. There are around three thousand people who openly spend this kind of money, but we estimate that there is an equal number of private buyers operating more discreetly, thus bringing the total of top-end art lovers, investors, dealer collectors, and corporate buyers to around six thousand people worldwide. This group is responsible for only a small number of total transactions in any given year, but the overall value represented by those transactions is huge. It is this group that is spending the majority of the money on the market—not in terms of volume but in terms of value.

Look at as much art as you can.
Jorge M. Pérez, Collector

In general, most art collectors are private buyers rather than corporate, and they are still, in the main, white men aged forty to sixty-four. Women collectors, however, are now on the rise (currently accounting for roughly 30%), and they seem to prefer contemporary art. As you might expect for the two regions with the largest share of the world's art galleries, the US and Europe are home to a collective 83% of the world's buyers, which explains why so many galleries are found there. For all galleries, local buyers are their most important clients. They may have developed an international presence, but it's still the buyers in their hometowns who generate revenue.

Learn from other collectors and collecting institutions, looking back and at the present. If you have another motivation for buying, for example market speculation, seek an advisor.
Cathy Leff, Curator

4.3.2
Positive and Negative Signs in the Market

An increase in the number of rich people is always the best possible news for the art market. Attendance numbers at exhibitions and shows increased too in recent years. In particular, the attendance at big art fairs such as Art

Basel has gone up, a good indicator of increased active interest in the art world.

Nonetheless, despite these positive indications, the number of artworks sold in the past decade has slightly dropped. Increasing visitor numbers and fewer sales lead to the conclusion that the art market has a conversion problem: people are coming to see art but are not buying. That's an important fact for you to understand, as this shows your negotiation power is larger than you might expect. In an industry where the number of clients who actually put their hands in their pockets is getting fewer every year, the power of those same clients increases. Remember this when you are negotiating your next art deal.

It's always quality over quantity. Never sit on your hands/pocket if it's a piece your heart beats for. Take the risk and go and get it.

Diandra Donecker, Auctioneer

4.4 Online Collectors

In light of falling conversion rates from visitors to buyers, optimism was high for a while that the online market would be a welcome savior. Dealers and gallerists hoped that a younger generation of new collectors would use remote technology to buy and, as a result, establish online channels as a firm revenue stream. Up until COVID-19 hit, they were continually disappointed. But in 2020 there was a rapid increase from 9% to 25% of the total market value. This figure has gone down again in 2021 and 2022 but is still above pre-pandemic levels, as collectors, dealers, artists, and auction houses, forced into remote transactions by world events, have become

Exercise your eye, do research, let your sensations guide you.

Patrizia Sandretto Re Rebaudengo, Collector

accustomed to an increase in digital interactions. Therefore, a very significant outcome of the pandemic and the changes it brought to the market is that it forced the art market, a previous e-commerce laggard, to catch up with other retail industries.

The real difference between the offline and online markets seems to be price. In annual expenditure terms, there is a sticking point of $10,000, with buyers hesitant to spend beyond that online. In fact, 76% spend less than $10,000, and 61% spend less than $5,000. Online buyers also tend to want more individual pieces for their money; they buy more artworks at lower prices, while offline collectors in the main (57%) spend the same sum on only one or two items. The future of online art sales seems uncertain, as 22% of buyers want to spend less money online and only about 30% want to increase their budget for online purchases.

The value of any artwork is comprised of both financial and nonfinancial value. When collectors acquire art from a gallery, they must realize that, generally, the fair market value will instantly be substantially lower than the retail price paid: FMV does not incorporate the nonfinancial or social value that art delivers in the primary market.

Chris Vroom, Collector

4.5 Collector Tools

One area where the art market lets itself down slightly is in offering tools that collectors can use to find, evaluate, and sell art. Most of the tools I suggest here lack the sophistication you might encounter in the financial industry, with its much broader and in many ways more democratized user base and its stricter regulations. Nonetheless, here are some news-gathering, price-checking, and what's-on tools that collectors use:

News

Staying in the know is very important in this industry, but you may have limited time. So here are the two most essential sites you should make time to scan. Most collectors I know subscribe to the Instagram accounts of and the free newsletter from these two companies:

Define a collecting thesis based on the people and stories you want to be told in the future. For me, that is artists and artworks that inspire authenticity. Joshua Pulman, Collector

- **Artnet News**
- **Artsy**

Both give you a great summary of what's going on in the international art world. Neither offers twenty-page reviews of art shows; instead, they deal in straightforward news from the art world, such as the highlights of recent or upcoming auctions, information on new artist representations by galleries, art-world gossip, lawsuits, and other dramas. It's entertaining and informative. Of all the outlets that are out there, these two are the most read by most art-world insiders.

Always buy two works by any artist you love. That way, if you have to sell one work, you'll still have another to enjoy forever. Nichole Galicia, Collector

Find Exhibitions

Going to exhibition openings is important. Two tools I use to find galleries and current shows:

- **See/Saw**
- **Artsy App**

More specifically, in Los Angeles, New York, London, Paris, and Berlin I use See/Saw, a free-to-download app that shows me all the openings for the week and has a feature for creating a map of shows I want to go to. The Artsy app, which is also free to download, provides a similar service. Plus you can read news, follow artists, and get alerts of upcoming events. If you are in a city that is not covered by these apps, there might be another app or website that covers that city. Googling "art shows" plus the name of your city will help you find a suitable app or website that lists all show openings. For example, searching for Miami will quickly lead you to the Instagram account @art.seen.365, which features daily openings.

Check Prices

Prices in the art world are notoriously secretive at the primary-market or gallery level, and despite my efforts to revolutionize this deficiency with technology (with an app that performs the same identification task as Shazam but for art), I ran up against considerable resistance. Prices in the secondary market, however, are transparent. There are several subscription services that show past auction results for an artist, determine whether a specific work was ever offered for sale at an auction and how much it sold for, find similar works by that artist so you can determine price ranges, and send email alerts when works by your artists are included in an upcoming auction. The biggest three are:

> **Collecting is a calling that finds you as a form of self-expression achieved through a mindfully curated and deeply intuitive pursuit of pieces that complete your story. Don't get distracted, greedy, or impressed over anything that doesn't fit your own personal puzzle.**
>
> Viera Gaon, Collector

- **Artnet**
- **LiveArt**
- **Artsy**

Artnet is the gold standard and charges a yearly subscription of less than $500. LiveArt is a newer solution and has less data but is free. Artsy, which is also free, is the only one that provides some (but not many) primary-market prices. You have nothing to lose if you register with LiveArt for auction results and Artsy for gallery prices, and I would recommend you do so.

Manage Your Inventory

I know you are at the start of your collection, and talking about managing an art inventory might feel a bit premature. But I still want to talk about it. Why? Because the number of collectors who don't have a grasp on the full scope of what they own is astonishing, and the associated paperwork (invoices, condition reports, etc.) also needs to be carefully stored. If you are buying one work, perhaps you don't need to think about collection management. But add one or two smaller purchases, perhaps of editions of bigger artists, and you are starting to form a collection. So at the very least, setting up an informal content-management system early on makes sense. Depending on your circumstances, I would go one of two ways:

- **A spreadsheet**
- **Artlogic, a cloud-based content-management system**

Looking at the formal content-management system first, companies such as Artlogic or ARTERNAL charge a monthly fee of between forty and eighty dollars. They are cloud-based services and allow access to your entire collection at your fingertips. You can also store your invoices, photos, condition reports, contacts at galleries, and any other information you may want to append in the same database. These services have quite extensive features, and their extended versions are often used by professional galleries, museums, and so on.

Collecting art can be a life-changing experience: to learn to think outside of the box, to move away from the handrail and the comfort of what we know to what we don't know yet, to open up to what is not us. Otherwise art collecting is just another speculative activity of accumulating other luxury goods for social status. When you are ready to understand this, go to museums and biennials as much as you can before going to art fairs; read or research online on the basis of what art is; try to find yourself a collector who can be your mentor, like I did, or listen to or read what he has to tell you. Start small, as mistakes are unavoidable, take your time, and challenge yourself every time. Alain Servais, Collector

This approach, though, is almost certainly overkill in the early years. A swift and highly informal survey of collector opinion on this suggested to me that these services come into their own once you have a hundred or more works. A far better solution when starting your collection is to track your works on a spreadsheet. Your sheet should include these columns:

- Image
- Item number
- Artist name
- Year when the artist finished it
- Title, medium, material, edition size, dimensions
- Location (Where is the piece now?)
- Purchase price
- Purchase date
- Vendor (gallery or auction house or directly from the artist)
- Status (loaned, donated, on consignment)
- Provenance (*Provenance* is another word for "exhibition and transaction history" of this work. If you buy from a gallery, it probably won't have a provenance, but if you bought it at an auction, this work may have been exhibited in museum shows, etc.)
- Condition (Here is where you record the details of any damage to the work when it passes into your hands or if unfortunate incidents happen after you have taken ownership. Trust me on this—it happens, and you won't always remember whether the damage happened on your watch or beforehand.)
- Notes, the final column, where you enter the classic miscellany common to all information-management systems.

Look at as much art as you can, read about it as much as possible, and ask as many questions as you can think of. This will shape your decisions. And avoid, or at least minimize, regret—always look forward! Ed Tang, Advisor

I personally still use a spreadsheet but know that I will soon be switching to a more convenient database solution as my collection keeps growing.

Case Study

ROSA AND CARLOS DE LA CRUZ—THE WORLD'S LAST ART LOVERS

Rosa and Carlos de la Cruz are two of the most beloved contemporary art collectors of our time. They first met as teenagers in Havana, Cuba, and married in 1962. Together they have amassed one of Miami's finest collections of modern art, including a notable smaller collection of postwar German paintings. They estimate their collection at more than five hundred works, almost all of which are on display either at their home in Key Biscayne or in their thirty-thousand-square-foot de la Cruz Collection Contemporary Art Space in Miami's Design District. Both are destinations during Art Basel Miami Beach each December.

Their collection started in the early 1980s with an initial focus on Latin American artists. As they showed me around their collection, Carlos told me that the first piece they acquired was *Star Gazer* (1956) by Rufino Tamayo. "When we bid on this work, we weren't even registered as bidders, so we had to borrow the paddle from friends who were with us in the auction room." Eventually, influenced by their lifelong friendship with Cuban artist Felix Gonzalez-Torres, they shifted their focus and purchased contemporary international artists. The collection now includes works by Mark Bradford, Peter Doig, Isa Genzken, Gonzalez-Torres, Albert Oehlen, Christopher Wool, and many other blue-chip artists.

Both at the museum and their Key Biscayne home, three things became clear to me. The first is that Rosa and Carlos are driven by ideas, not by money. They purchase works only after a careful discourse with the work and the artists. "What is important to us are the ideas artists are communicating and how we connect with their work. New acquisitions should be in conversation with works that we already own." The hours I (very happily) spent in their company showed that this sentiment is absolutely sincere, and a badly needed corrective in a world where collecting is widely, if not exclusively, associated with investing. They are infinitely knowledgeable about the artists they collect, conversations with them never flag, and they never refer to money or the market.

Secondly, their focus is entirely on the best works by the artists. "We try to purchase only those works that we consider to be the best, independent from what the market thinks." This gives them an enviable discipline. Collectors on their level are bombarded with offers from gallerists and artists. If you don't learn to say no, you can easily end up with a collection of more than ten thousand works, most of which end up in storage. Rosa and Carlos made a clear decision to stay focused; they don't have storage—almost all the works they own are on their walls.

And thirdly, they collect because they have a larger ambition: to support artists and their local community. They organize lectures, offer scholarships to high school students, and pay for educational travel to Europe for college students, even providing suitcases so students don't need to worry about travel expenses. Moreover, unlike many private museums that exist partly to reduce tax liabilities, the de la Cruz Collection is entirely self-funded with no government grants.

The de la Cruz partnership fits my description of art lovers to perfection because of their passion-based motivation to buy.

ADVICE

It is important to do your homework before purchasing and follow the artist's trajectory afterward. The particular work should be an important one for the artist and should be compatible with the other works with which it will be installed.

5
Artists

—Selecting Artists to Collect

As a collector, your most important counterpart is the artist. And as a new collector, the sheer number of artists—now at an all-time high, and still rising—can be overwhelming. Joseph Beuys was right when he said everyone can be an artist—you don't need either official qualifications or even proven attendance at an art college, and those attracted by the impression of high rewards in contemporary art and possessing enough self-confidence can proclaim themselves artists completely unchallenged.

5.1 Overview and Classification

In an industry that lacks objective criteria to define what good art is, it's difficult for collectors to decide what artist to buy. Some artists, even talented ones, fall by the wayside, and others may be hidden superstars whose rise to fame is yet to come. I want to help you navigate through the sheer oversupply of artists by showing you where an artist falls in our groupings.

> Collecting art requires real passion. In that context, the term "value" is primarily not an economic one. Collecting naturally requires funds. The fun of it, however—making bold moves by combining different positions—is its essence and brings in your personal touch.
>
> Leopold Weinberg, Collector

Categorization of artist type is not a precise science, but the table below illustrates the breakdown of artist types using the five divisions that I set out in our Artist Framework earlier. While there can be frequent and rapid movement between categories at the outset of artists' careers (for example, an early and successful move from the high-street to the mature and emerging tier), these classifications—as I discussed earlier when I outlined gallery categories and their effect on an artist's career—become essentially set in stone within a few years of starting to exhibit.

> Hold your anxiety and take your time before your purchase, because art is for life.
>
> Sofia Derani, Collector

- **Superstars: 0.5%**
- **Mature and Emerging Artists: 6%**
- **High-Street Artists: 12%**
- **Vanity Artists: 40%**
- **Passion Artists: 41.5%**

DISTRIBUTION OF ARTISTS

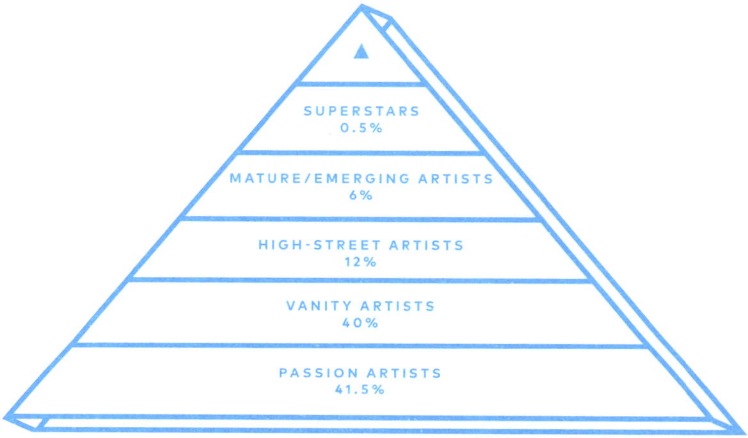

SOURCE: RESCH, 2011

Superstar Artists

Superstar artists are essentially the extended list of the top fifty most important contemporary artists. They have eight-figure incomes, create the premium lots at major evening auctions, and hold single-artist shows at global top museums. Their works are in the collections of top museums and collectors, and various catalogues of their works have been produced by respected publishers. These are artists such as David Hockney, Gerhard Richter, and Christopher Wool. In essence, these are the household names that line the walls of the biggest art museums in the world.

> **There is no right way to go through an art museum. I would argue: there is no right way to collect art. Let yourself be directed by your emotions and the flow, just like when you walk through a museum.**
>
> Zeki Sever, Collector

Mature and Emerging Artists

Mature and emerging artists have a great reputation and stable sales records, with a slightly lower income of around seven figures. Their works are included in top auctions but take second place to the superstars. They have probably participated in group shows at top museums but have had single-artist shows only at regional institutions. Their works are still collected by museums and important collectors, but catalogues are distributed nationwide instead of globally. Examples of these artists would be Marilyn Minter and Ugo Rondinone.

Lean into the inspiring future of how art is evolving. Embrace new mediums, tools, and modalities of art in an open-minded fashion. Ryan Zurrer, Collector

High-Street Artists

High-street artists are local stars with national recognition but who are internationally unknown. They typically have a five-, maybe six-figure income and a small presence on the secondary market. They participate in group shows in national museums and are represented by local galleries, who publish catalogues for them.

Vanity Artists

Vanity artists have little to no reputation and make a small income through art that requires supplementing, often with teaching. They are completely absent from the secondary market and may have varying representation by local galleries. Catalogues of their work, if any, are usually self-published.

Only buy (or build) what you love. Never use art as investment. The odds of turning a profit are very low, so be ready to sit with your acquisition forever. Tom Sachs, Artist

Passion Artists

Passion artists are the most common and have no reputation within the art world. They do not make an income through art, although they may seek representation. They are completely outside both the primary and secondary markets. They may organize exhibitions by themselves or through friends and have no catalogues of their work.

5.2 Career Stages

CAREER PROGRESSION OF THE DIFFERENT TYPES OF ARTIST

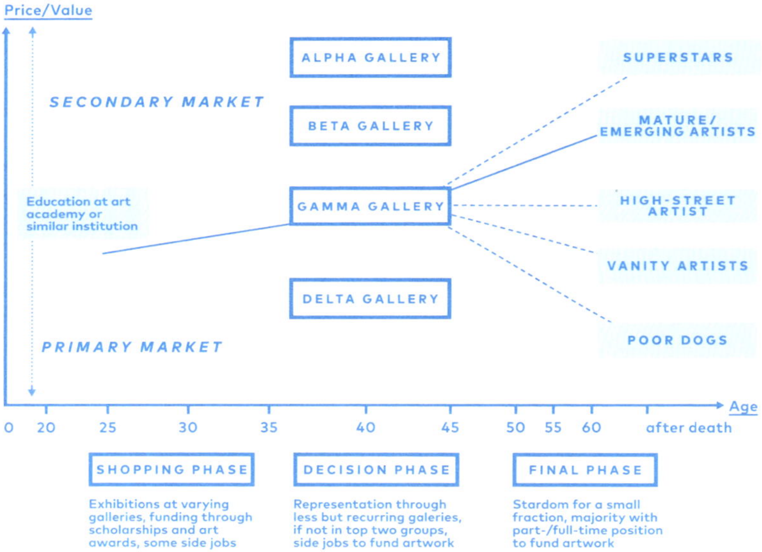

Bearing in mind the five categories of artist in the Artist Framework, I want to zoom in on the career path an artist takes. Their career can usually be separated into three phases: the shopping phase, the decision phase, and the final phase.

The shopping phase is characterized by young artists with long exhibition records showing at varying galleries. They work extremely hard, they are funded by scholarships, and they hope to be spotted by an alpha or beta gallery. This phase extends from the moment an artist graduates (if they went to art school) until roughly age thirty-five. It's the phase when it's hardest for collectors to identify what path the artist is taking, as artists experiment with various galleries, and their classification is in flux. In this initial shopping phase, artists will build networks and will try their best to self-promote. At this stage, very few will get into an alpha gallery; most will exhibit in beta to delta galleries first. Very rarely will an artist have a solo show at this stage, but they will likely participate in group shows.

Sharpen your eye by seeing as many exhibitions as possible: Picasso, Mondrian, O'Keeffe, and all the greatest. But at the same time, be courageous and try to buy the next generation's Picasso early. Andreas Ritter, Collector

In this phase, those without an art education might start a career as a freelance artist. They start off exhibiting their work in mostly noncommercial spaces and reach a greater audience. Artist-curated shows are organized by fellow artists who use their own networks to invite potential customers. This kind of initiative has led to the emergence of producer galleries, in which artists act as both agent and gallery manager, taking on responsibility for renting a gallery, promoting, and selling. Artist-curated shows, as well as producer galleries, provide the artists with crucial exposure for both better representation and for sales.

Make sure you love what you collect. Do not get consumed by the economy of art and lose sight of its true purpose.
George Merck, Collector

At the end of this stage, artists would hope to have moved to superstar or mature and emerging status, defined by the tier of gallery that represents them. Bigger artists will be represented by alpha or beta galleries and will remain at this level for the rest of their career.

The decision phase is made up of slightly older artists, around the age of thirty-five, who have found their role in the art market and their representation (or not). In this phase it becomes easier for collectors to differentiate between individual artists. By looking at the galleries where the artist shows, collectors can gain a good understanding of their classification level.

At the beginning of this phase, artists will usually have shown at various galleries. A very small fraction who came through the shopping phase with the right kind of exposure are able to engage in closer relationships with alpha or beta galleries and thus pursue superstar or mature and emerging status. The great majority, sadly, stagnate in gamma or delta galleries, or they are dropped altogether. Two in five new artists will no longer be showing in a gamma gallery five years after their first show, two will have been marginally successful, and only one will be moderately profitable for the gallery. Those who leave will either find new representation with another comparable gallery or will drop to a delta gallery. The overlap between these artists and those in the bottom three tiers of artist status—high-street, vanity, and passion—is pretty much 100%, and these artists will be almost completely funded by their secondary jobs rather than their artistic practices.

Collect art from artists showing a compelling long-term vision and profound narrative. These are the creators who will continue making high-profile art and innovating regardless of market conditions. Andrea Bonaceto, Collector

In the **final phase**, the artist's status becomes obvious. This phase also sees a great percentage of artists abandoning full-time work as artists, with only a tiny number actually making a living from it and maintaining a presence on the art market, even after death.

The final phase begins at the age of roughly forty-five, by which time a very small fraction of artists is represented by an alpha or beta gallery. They are comfortable financially, with up to eight-figure revenues at the highest end. Through national Kunsthallen and major biennials in Western Europe, mature and emerging artists will still hope for passage to superstar ranking, with work dealt in both primary and secondary markets. Superstars, of course, will be featured in frequent solo shows around the world and will continue to be shown and traded during their lifetime and after their death.

Ask questions, and make sure you believe in the story and the artist behind the works.
Charlie Jarvis, Art Tech Founder

During this phase, though, the remainder—the overwhelming majority—do not make a living from their art and are unlikely still accessing scholarships or other funding possibilities. They will either continue to practice side by side with other paid work or they will relinquish their artistic career altogether.

Art is not mashed potato. Try to challenge yourself and buy artists from your own generation.
Patricia Marshall, Advisor

5.3 Artist Data

It's hard to calculate how many artists exist, as the definition of who is an artist is so broad, but if we counted the number of artists who are exhibiting their works in for-profit or not-for-profit institutions on any given day, worldwide, there would be roughly 180,000 artists. If you were to then add those who are not exhibiting on the day of such a theoretical census—because they will exhibit some other time this year or they don't have representation—we would easily reach one million artists or more.

We can say more confidently that there are roughly seventy thousand gallery and museum exhibitions per year all over the world. Of these, 23% take place in the US, making it the world's leading country for exhibitions, followed by the UK and France. Australia and South America each represent 3% of total global exhibitions. The number of exhibitions that China hosts yearly has doubled over the past five years but still accounts for only 2% of total exhibitions worldwide. Collectively, Asia represents 5% of global exhibitions.

Follow your heart. Only buy what you love—especially if your purchase will help the artist directly.
Suzanne Delehanty, Advisor

Comparing exhibition figures with sales figures, there is no real geographic correlation: the US, UK, and China dominate with 84% of sales but collectively host only 31% of exhibitions. In other words, while sales are highly concentrated within three countries, exhibitions are everywhere.

Do not think about collecting. Become engaged. See, meet, listen, feel, and learn. Then acquire a work of art that touches your eyes, your mind, and your heart.
Dakis Joannou, Collector

When it comes to the artists exhibited in national galleries, there is a strong preference for homegrown talent: a German institution prefers to show a German artist, a US institution an American artist, and so on.

Predictably, superstars are far and away the most widely exhibited contemporary artists. Andy Warhol has held the no. 1 spot for the past decade, followed by Picasso at no. 2. The third, fourth, and fifth spots have changed annually between the same three artists: Bruce Nauman, Gerhard Richter, and Joseph Beuys.

5.4 How to Select the Right Artist

By this point, it's very clear that there is an oversupply of exhibitions and artists. For any collector, but particularly new ones, this can be confusing, making it difficult to select an artist. The idea behind this systematic and categorized approach is to help you identify the artist, or at least artist type, you are looking for. It also helps you estimate a price point, verify investment potential, and compare your selected artist to other artists.

The next step is to demonstrate how to put this into practice so that you can fly solo in selecting the right artist. I have a tried-and-trusted route below, which I've used with my students and with collectors who have consulted me.

5·4·1
Step 1: Request a Biography

Whenever you are interested in any artist, you will first need to study her biography or CV (curriculum vitae) in order to find out which classification she's in. In practical terms, this means doing some internet research: check her website or the website of the gallery that represents her. Anytime you are in a gallery with interesting artists, always ask for biographies—it's pretty much the first thing I do as soon as I walk into any gallery. You'll normally find printed copies of both the CV and any press articles on the reception desk or can access them via a QR code, but if not, don't be shy about asking: interested visitors are always welcome visitors for gallerists.

5·4·2
Step 2: Apply Our Classification Criteria

Once you have the biography in front of you, try to work out which level fits the artist. A quick reminder of the criteria:

- **Representation:** What kind of gallery represents her? This is the most important and the most obvious criterion. As we know, there are alpha, beta, gamma, and delta galleries, and their status defines the artist's status. With younger artists, who tend to transfer from gallery to gallery, make sure you have the most up-to-date CV, including the most recent shows and the latest gallery relationships.

Don't confuse art with morality.
Caspar Jopling, Gallerist

- **Exhibitions:** Which institutions have offered her solo exhibitions? What is her history with group exhibitions? What do the dates of her exhibiting history tell you about her trajectory? While current gallery representation is critical, take a closer look at other exhibitions in the artist's history—for example, at other galleries or other museums. My research has shown that exhibitions, and particularly the stature of the institution hosting the exhibition, have an enormous impact on the success of an artist. Consider not only the exhibiting institution but also the year the exhibition was held and the level of individual exposure for the artist—in other words, was it a group show or the more valuable solo show?

You must first educate your eye to see the qualities that make an artist great: go to museums and galleries and talk to artists. Only then study markets, build access, and make soul-enriching decisions. Lauren Prakke, Collector

▸ **Collections:** What collections is she in? Do you recognize any big museum or collector names? While the fact that an artist is exhibiting demonstrates that the host institution is backing them, institutional commitment toward an artist can also be inferred from inclusion in the collection of the organization, whether a museum (look for branded names) or a known art collector or celebrity. A work held in a celebrity collection will generally have more value: a Warhol that was part of the Yves Saint Laurent collection, for example, will sell for considerably more than a similar Warhol that was part of an unknown collection. The provenance of the work is a major factor in value. Exhibition exposure at a museum does not necessarily lead to a place in its collection, nor is the reverse true. Artists may enter a museum's collection because of a donation, for example, but their work may never actually hang there. They will still benefit, however, from inclusion in the museum's listed collection.

Collect from the heart because you want to wake up in the morning feeling good about what you have done.

Robert Chambers, Artist

▸ **Bibliography:** Have any leading publishers released a monograph (a publication detailing her biography), putting the artist's works and career to date in context? Has the press paid much attention to her? Which magazines have written about her?

While this indicator has suffered from diminishing relevance with each passing year, to those who are traditionally minded in the art world, it still matters if, for example, the *New York Times* has reviewed an artist's show or if your book was published by Walther König, and so on. What you need to interrogate here is the relevance—or perhaps, in today's terms, the influencer value—of any magazine that has written about the artist.

▸ **Auction Results:** How many auction results are there to draw on? What is the gap between the initial estimate and the actual sale price? When were those auctions?

Auction results are a good indicator of the price level and traction this artist enjoys in the market. I use the LiveArt free app to review the artist. Particularly, I look at how many auction results I can find for the artist. If an artist has no auction results, it makes it highly unlikely that I will ever be able to resell the work. The value of the work I am about to buy—just to drive home the point—is zero. Since very few artists ever get as far as the secondary (auction) market, this is by far the most likely outcome. Five auction results in the past two years is a good benchmark to show that there is some liquidity in the market. I also look closely at the gap between the estimate (the price the auction house thinks the work is worth) and the actual price at which the hammer drops. If an artist has repeatedly sold for less than the estimate, then the market is clearly not attractive. Finally, I check the date of the last few trades. If there haven't been any sales in the past two years, again, the market might not be attractive.

To have a collection and watch certain artists rise is such a joy. Then you know that your investment has grown. But no matter what, the joy that art brings to your home is priceless.

Brian Whiteley, Art Fair Founder

These are not particularly difficult or complicated ideas in themselves, but putting them into practice might still feel a bit hard to visualize. In the next section, I'm going to apply all these suggestions, step by step, to a few existing artists to give you an idea of how to actually follow these directions when you are looking at your new biography of any artist. Scanning the artist's CV, once you have got your eye in, is going to be less than a minute's work.

5.4.3
Applying It in Practice

SUPERSTAR ARTIST: JEFF KOONS

PACE

Jeff Koons
Born 1955, York, Pennsylvania
Lives and works in New York

Education
1976 BFA, Maryland Institute College of Art, Baltimore

Solo Exhibitions
2022 Pace, Palm Beach, Florida
2021 Palazzo Strozzi, Florence, Italy
2018 Gagosian, New York
2014 Whitney Museum of American Art, New York. Traveled to Centre Pompidou, Paris; Guggenheim Museum, Bilbao, Spain

Group Exhibitions
2007 MoMA P.S.1, New York
2000 Museum of Modern Art, New York

Collections
Museum of Modern Art, New York
Whitney Museum of American Art, New York
Tate Modern, London

Bibliography
2022 *New York Times*
2022 *Wall Street Journal*
2022 *Vanity Fair*

Representation: From his biography you can immediately see that Jeff Koons is represented by Pace gallery, one of the leading alpha galleries in the world. Previously, he was with Gagosian and has also shown with David Zwirner—all alpha galleries. We immediately know that this artist is a superstar artist.

Exhibitions: As with most biographies of artists, this divides his shows into solo exhibitions and group exhibitions. In this case, you can see that he has had solo shows at alpha galleries and at household-name museums, such as the Whitney and Centre Pompidou, plus he participated in group shows in museums such as MoMA. Based on our framework, you know that this artist's works will be expensive.

Coffins don't have pockets.
Ellie Rines, Gallerist

Collections: Often, when you look at the bottom of the CV, you can see which collections, public and private, hold works by the artist. As you can see, Koons's work is part of some of the most important art collections in the world, including MoMA, the Whitney, and many others.

Bibliography: The bibliography section includes a summary of press articles or publications about the artist. This section is often found below or above the collections. In Koons's case, to no surprise, he has had a lot of press in the leading newspapers globally and books published by the best publishers in the world.

Auction Results: The last step is to review auction prices via the LiveArt app. With the worldwide record price for a living artist—$91 million for *Rabbit* in 2019—Koons clearly shows exceptional auction results. LiveArt will also tell you that he has an extremely healthy set of more than five hundred results on the secondary market.

David Zwirner

Oscar Murillo
Born 1986, La Paila, Colombia
Lives and works in various locations

Education
2012 MFA, Royal College of Art, London
2007 BFA, University of Westminster, London

Solo Exhibitions
2014 David Zwirner, New York
2012 Rubell Family Collection, Miami
2011 Carlos/Ishikawa, London

Group Exhibitions
2013 David Zwirner, New York

Collections
Museum of Modern Art, New York
Museum of Contemporary Art, Los Angeles
Museum Ludwig, Cologne, Germany

Bibliography
2021 *New York Times*
2019 *New York Times*
2015 *New York Times*

Representation: Oscar Murillo shows with David Zwirner, an alpha gallery. He has been showing with them since 2013, so he is firmly embedded as a part of Zwirner's set of represented artists. This immediately positions Murillo as a superstar artist.

Exhibitions: Murillo has had shows with David Zwirner and museums around the world. His earlier career is all laid out in his biographical details above, and although he is now a superstar, his early years form an excellent study in how to spot an artist who is on the rise and shows great investment potential. As we discussed before, look for artists who are still under the age of thirty-five, who haven't shown much but are being included in group shows in alpha galleries, and who have some market traction evidenced by solid auction results. Murillo was at this point in 2012 and 2013, and they were the game-changing years of his career.

Many artists collaborate with others. So when you buy one artist's work, you may get access to art from other artists in their network too. Nicole Ianniello, Advisor

The Rubells, a couple living in Miami, whose interview you can find in my online class, are known to be the world's leading collectors in discovering upcoming emerging artists. In 2012 they gave Murillo a solo show at their museum, which put him firmly on the map. Had you been following my directions in 2012, it would have been the signal for you, as a collector, to take note, as Murillo fulfilled all the characteristics of an artist to watch. In 2012 he was only twenty-six years old, had just graduated from London's Royal College of Art, and had only participated in a few shows. He had not yet been picked up by an alpha gallery. Only a few months later, in early 2013, he was invited to show with the alpha gallerist David Zwirner in a group show. Inviting a young artist to a group show is a preferred way for alpha galleries to find out what it's like to work with the artist and get an idea of collector appetite for their work, much like giving a young footballer a tryout with the team. Following the career graphic of artists included earlier in this book, which introduced the concept of the shopping phase, the group show at Zwirner was the decisive moment in Murillo's shopping phase that catapulted him from

Seek out experts, whether it's an advisor, curator, writer, or gallerist. So much of contemporary art is hard to understand without some context, and the art market is notoriously opaque. It is helpful to have an expert guide you through what you are seeing and considering.

Kelly Huang, Advisor

showing with beta and gamma galleries to showing with an alpha gallery, introducing him to the superstar league and lifelong success. A surprise result at Christie's in 2014 also saw one of his works sell for six times the estimate, at $320,000, an unmistakable indication of Murillo's rise. From that point, his career was made. Today, his works sell for $500,000 and higher.

If you can, and have the liquidity, take some risks—think of collecting as a learning experience and allow yourself to make mistakes. Adam Lindemann, Collector

Collections: Murillo is in a large number of museum collections, including branded names such as MoMA; the Museum of Contemporary Art, Los Angeles; and Museum Ludwig, Cologne. Compared to Koons, the number of collections is fewer, and their reputation is lower.

Bibliography: A variety of newspapers, including the *New York Times*, have written about him. As a young artist with a short exhibition history, his press history (which may need to be fully researched with a Google search rather than relying on his CV) is fairly short, with about ten entries, compared to that of the older Koons, who numbers more than one hundred articles.

Buy with your heart and eyes first, and if you are super compelled by those, buy the biggest, best example you can! Ignore where it might go; a new sofa is cheaper than missing an amazing opportunity for an artwork that will give you inspiration and joy for years.
Jeremy Kost, Artist

Auction Results: A check on Murillo's auction results shows around 150 auction trades in the past two years, so he is clearly an artist with an active and healthy trading performance. He hasn't yet reached the Koons level, with no results in the seven-digit area.

SALON 94

Marilyn Minter
Born 1948, Shreveport, California
Lives and works in New York

Education
1972 MFA, Syracuse University, Syracuse, New York
1970 BFA, University of Florida, Gainesville

Solo Exhibitions
2023 LGDR, New York
2021 Lehmann Maupin, Beijing
2018 Regen Projects, Los Angeles
2016 Salon 94 Bowery, New York
2010 Museum of Modern Art, New York

Group Exhibitions
2006 Whitney Museum of American Art, New York

Collections
Guggenheim Museum, New York
Tate Modern, London
Museum of Modern Art, New York
Whitney Museum of American Art, New York

Bibliography
2019 *New York Times*
2018 *New York Times Magazine*
1995 *New York Times*

Representation: From Marilyn Minter's biography and personal website we can see that she is represented by Salon 94 and Regen Projects. These are both beta galleries. (I will return to galleries and their classifications and explain how to analyze their status in the Galleries chapter.) It's not uncommon for an artist to be represented by more than one gallery, as each will represent Minter in one region exclusively. In this case, Salon 94 represents her in NYC, while in LA she is represented by Regen Projects. Neither gallery has representation in the other city, and Minter's collector base seems to be strong in both. In Asia, she partners with Lehmann Maupin, which has a strong presence there. The information available suggests that she has had a long relationship with these galleries and has shown with them for many years.

Find things that you connect with. Things that elicit an emotional response that you can't

Exhibitions: A quick scan of her CV for branded institutions shows that she participated in a solo show at MoMA and in a group show at the Whitney Museum. She has also participated in various other solo and group shows. Clearly, she has had a long career. Compared to Koons, we see that the frequency of solo shows in the best museums and galleries is less.

Collections: Given her extensive exhibition history, Minter is unsurprisingly included in a wide range of collections, including top global institutions such as MoMA and the Guggenheim.

Bibliography: We can see that she has an extensive bibliography with many leading magazines having written about her. Compared to Koons, Minter's coverage in top magazines is smaller. While it's hard to spot this immediately when looking at a paper summary, a quick Google search will show that the *New York Times* has written more than one hundred times about Koons and fewer than forty times about Minter. Minter has still received more coverage than Murillo, but with an age difference of forty years, this is likely the consequence of a longer career.

Auction Results: With around two hundred entries, she has less than half of Koons's entries, which might also reflect the fact that she produces fewer works. We can clearly see that her market is active, yet price points are considerably lower than Koons's for original pieces. Her top prices are in the range of $300,000 and have never reached a seven-digit figure.

JACKIE MERRIHAM

Sara Douglas
Born 1951, Atlanta
Lives and works in Berlin

Education
1974 University of California, Los Angeles
1969 Art Academy, New York

Solo Exhibitions
2017 Betty Cuningham Gallery, New York
2008 Galleria Fantastico, Turin, Italy

Group Exhibitions
2016 Christian Beveres Gallery, New York
2000 Galleria Architettura, Milan

Grants
2005 Adolph and Esther Friedhelm Foundation
2001 Polack-Krausnic Foundation

Collections
Museum of Contemporary Art Atlanta
German Institute, New York
Bank of America, Los Angeles

Representation: Sara Douglas (a pseudonym to protect her privacy) is represented by Jackie Merriham Gallery (pseudonym), a gamma gallery. This immediately tells us that this artist is neither a superstar nor an emerging/mature artist: a gamma gallery will show main-street, vanity, or passion artists. To identify the exact classification and its corresponding price level, a further look is necessary.

Exhibitions: Douglas has a great and substantial list of exhibitions, but neither her solo nor her group shows are in the world's leading museums or galleries, placing her in the island network. As with many artists so situated, she has frequently exhibited internationally, which has had no impact on her success level. International exposure sets up one of the most common traps for potential collectors: international showing, in fact, has no significance for an artist's status or career. Douglas has also received various grants.

Context is king. An artwork is a representation of an artist's wider practice. You should fall in love with the wider practice as well as the object.
Magnus Renfrew, Art Fair Founder

Grants are often a way for artists to finance their work, as are teaching positions. These have little or no impact on the classification of an artist, and I don't include them in my evaluation of an artist.

Collections: Douglas is in various museum collections, but none of the institutions are part of the Holy Land discussed earlier in this book. To reiterate, only a few institutions are part of the Holy Land in which value is created. Beyond that, even large collections such as the Bank of America or a public collection such as the Museum of Contemporary Art in Atlanta have little impact on the success level of an artist.

Bibliography: She has received some coverage but none in international media, and mostly in local newspapers.

Auction Results: Investigations show two auction results, and they are from more than five years ago. In her case, the results are from Christie's, which is an alpha auction house, but since the results are so few and so old, there is clearly no solid secondary market for her work. In turn, that means that if you wanted to sell a Sara Douglas, you would almost certainly not be able to.

Listen, learn, and read as much as you are able but buy with your eyes, not your ears. You must look hard and look long. And if you truly love what you buy, you will never make a mistake.
Adam Weinberg, Museum Director

GALLERY ZAR

Petr Mayer
Born 1971, Dallas, Texas
Lives and works in Montreal

Education
1999 BS, Marketing, University of Texas

Solo Exhibitions
2020 Red See Lodge, Park City, Utah
2019 Firedance Art Studio, Dallas, Texas
2018 Window House, Austin, Texas

Grants
2020 Springsteen Museum of Art, Texas
2018 Merchant Bank Art Show, Texas

Collections
Hotel Jackson, Dallas, Texas
The Lodge, Austin, Texas

Representation: Petr Mayer (again, the name has been changed) is represented by Gallery Zar (pseudonym), a delta gallery located in Dallas, Texas. Jumping forward to the Galleries chapter, you will see that all alpha and beta galleries are located in major art cities (and most in New York City), telling you immediately that the gallery cannot be alpha or beta. From here, you can guess that the artist will be a vanity or passion artist.

Exhibitions: His exhibition overview is rather short, probably because art is not his main source of income. None of the shows is in a leading gallery or museum. Even without knowing the galleries in question, their locations give you an idea of their classification. As with the high-street artist Sara Douglas,

Mayer also won some awards but from banks or other business institutions that support artists rather than from leading institutions.

Collections: Mayer is in various collections but none held by leading art museums or important collectors. Often for artists at this level, collections are held by hotels or by lesser known art collectors in locations far from the main art hubs.

Bibliography: His works have been covered in various magazines and newspapers, including the *LA Times* and *Mountain Living Magazine*, but there are no catalogues about the artist.

Auction Results: There are no auction results available for this artist, so there is no resale market for his works.

PASSION ARTIST: TRISHA WEISSMAN

Trisha Weissman

Trisha Weissman
Born 1977, Berlin
Lives and works in Paris

No art education
No listed solo and group shows
Active Instagram account

Representation: Our final artist, whom we have called Trisha Weissman, doesn't have a CV listed on her website, nor is one available when Googling her. No gallery representation can be found for her. If she is selling, she's selling directly to clients through her Instagram and website.

Exhibitions: No exhibitions are listed on her website.

Collections: No collections are listed.

Bibliography: No press articles or catalogues are listed.

Auction Results: When I Googled her, I couldn't find any auction results.

5·4·4 Summary

I have shown you how you can select artists based on the groupings we have developed. It's important to be aware of the classification of the artist you are getting involved with, as it has a direct impact on their price level and future resale value and opportunity. For a vanity artist such as Mayer, you need to know that when you pay $50,000 for a work, you will almost certainly never see that money again. And if you buy from an artist like Douglas, you should do so with the understanding that you are very unlikely to see a price increase in her work, or see her work in the collection of the MoMA.

Don't try to get a deal. They don't exist. Buy the best quality that you can afford. If you are suffering to buy an artwork, you are probably buying very well. In case of doubt, call me.
Loïc Gouzer, Advisor

Having some knowledge when you navigate the art market should help you to feel more confident when buying art—and, equally important, feel good about spending the money because you can go in with a clear understanding of what it's worth.

The really paradoxical thing about art, and in my view one of the most important things to appreciate, is that while superstar and emerging/mature artists are at the top of the pyramid, their art isn't necessarily any better in any form than that of main-street, vanity, or passion artists. Their art might be better from an investment viewpoint, but we have learned

Bringing a piece of art into your home is saying, "I want to live with you. I want to see you every day." It should feel romantic, and a little bit thrilling. For me, I prefer art with a story—something I'm excited to share when people visit. Andi Potamkin, Collector

that only a few artists really serve as an investment. So main-street, vanity, and passion artists are all great artists who you can and should collect with as much enthusiasm as a more famous artist—if you feel a connection to their work. I buy from each of these categories without hesitation because they are as passionate and hard-working, and they love what they are doing. Their art is by no means bad art, and taste is highly subjective.

Don't buy early. Buying from art school MFA open houses often means buying work that is premature. Instead, create a framework for the collection that will serve as your guide while you see art. Erin Jenoa Gilbert, Advisor

If you want to chat and are not sure about the artist you are considering buying, please do reach out. You can book 1:1 sessions with me via magnusclass.com, and I will consult you in the buying process.

5·4·5
Dos and Don'ts

Dos

- **Look at the CV first.**
- **Scan the CV for alpha institutions.**
- **Ask galleries and artists about prices.**

Don'ts

- **Don't be shy: if you can't find the CV, ask for it.**
- **Don't be shy to ask for the price either.**
- **Don't overpay because you think you have spotted the next Basquiat. The chances are incredibly low.**
- **Don't think that high-street, vanity, or passion artists are bad artists. Good art and bad art is so subjective as to make value judgments meaningless. If you like something, it's great art.**

Case Study

TAVARES STRACHAN—HOW TO FLY TO THE MOON

Tavares Strachan has been considered an emerging star on the global art scene the past few years. In 2022 he received the MacArthur "Genius Grant," probably the most important prize in the world that an artist can win, and he is shown by leading galleries globally. Among Strachan's works are a gold bust of Robert Henry Lawrence Jr., the first Black American astronaut, which Strachan sent into space (with the aid of Elon Musk's SpaceX); the transportation of a 4.5-ton ice block from Alaska to the Bahamas (with the aid of FedEx); and the development of a clothing line (with the aid of his mother). His fascinating story maps closely to the different phases shown in my artist's career graphic.

Strachan was born in Nassau, Bahamas, in 1979, the second of six boys. His mother was a dressmaker and his father was a police officer and administrator. "We were poor, but we didn't know it." He eventually attended Rhode Island School of Design (RISD) to pursue an education as an artist, but every campus job opening he could find wasn't enough to keep up with his fees. When the provost informed him that he would have to leave if he couldn't pay, he negotiated fervently to remain, which required him to find a determination that was almost as transformative in developmental terms as the art education he received: "They repeatedly said 'no' before responding 'yes.'" Finally, RISD provided the funding he required to remain, a wise decision now fully justified by the high-profile Strachan's membership on the board of trustees. He moved on to study at Yale School of Art and graduated with an MFA in 2006.

After leaving Yale, Strachan entered the shopping phase. During this time he showed with more than ten galleries around the world, mostly gamma galleries. In 2013 he had his breakthrough, at the Venice Biennale, the world's oldest and most prestigious recurrent art exhibition, where he represented the Bahamas in its first-ever national pavilion. In what I would describe as the decision phase, larger galleries then took notice. He showed at Art Basel with beta gallery Anthony Meier Fine Arts and participated in solo shows with Fergus McCaffrey and Regen Projects. In 2020 he finally signed with Marian Goodman Gallery and Perrotin, both galleries that are leading the beta-gallery segment.

With the support of these top beta galleries, his career has taken another upward turn. In 2023 he showed at Centre Pompidou and the Museum of Contemporary Art Chicago, and in 2024 he will have solo exhibitions at Los Angeles County Museum of Art and London's Hayward Gallery.

Strachan's story is a good illustration of an artist moving through the career stages. It also shows that sometimes the career of an artist may require more than five or ten exhibitions to take off, provided those exhibitions take place at the right locations. Now in the decision phase of his career, Tavares will continue on his skyward trajectory. He is represented by a beta gallery, and I am sure, with a solid show history behind him, he will soon join the alpha ranks. His career has just begun to boom.

ADVICE

I grew up poor, with not much art in my house at all. So in some ways I am the worst person to answer this question. The thing is, the industry is filled with folks who are good at telling you what you should think and be interested in. This phenomenon is probably not unique to the art world. Honestly, the most important thing is to buy what you like. Even when moving into a new discipline, your instincts are still critical to your survival and success. No serious human should give up their own point of view to end up with art that someone else told them they should have. See everything and go toward what moves you first; become educated about it and look to form a deeper connection with the work. This way the work will become a part of you and your story and enrich your experience.

6
Galleries

—Finding a Partner You Can Trust

The simplest day-to-day definition of *gallerist* is a commercial intermediary selling art so that artists can produce more work. But there is a lot more to the gallerist role than just sales. Gallery owners identify artists, support and nurture them, and promote them to collectors, writers, and curators. They must be talent spotters, advocates, and publicists, and they need to be good at those roles if their artists are to succeed. For investing collectors, the quality of your gallerist is paramount. When we discussed artist classifications, it was clear that while the scarcity of buyers puts potential collectors in a strong position, gallerists command huge influence over what a collector may eventually buy—they are the gatekeepers of the art world. Not only do they have a great deal of power over artists' fates, but they also have some power over yours as a collector.

6.1 Overview and Classification

Artists and collectors may seem like the only truly crucial players in the art market, but gallerists play a critical role as facilitators between the two. Surprisingly, given their central role in facilitating the art market, most gallery owners have no particular business education, as running a gallery requires no additional qualifications than any other form of retail. This may, incidentally, explain the average gallery owner's resistance to contracts and written agreements.

If you have the opportunity before buying, look at any and all works available. There are often gems hidden in studios and previous bodies of work.

Kathryn Mikesell, Collector

Among the more high-profile galleries, the revenue model may be two-sided, with the gallery active on both the primary and secondary markets. But as a whole, the majority are active only in the primary market, where revenue comes mainly from selling works by artists represented by the gallery. Usually the gallery and the artist will split the revenue fifty-fifty (minus the cost of production). If the artist is sold by one gallery but represented by another, the gallery that formally represents the artist will usually get a 10% commission. In this market, prices are subject to negotiation; typically an initial price is agreed upon by the artist and the selling gallery, but discounts may be given to museums or known collectors with enough influence to raise the profile, and hence selling power, of the artist.

Surround yourself with smart, trustworthy, and passionate people who care about the quality of the art, and have fun doing your own research!

Jaclyn Lavy, NFT Specialist

A small, select group of galleries is also active on the secondary market, either buying on behalf of the collectors they represent or for the gallery's inventory. They may also act as an investor collector, trying to buy undervalued works to resell at a higher price. Finally, they might attempt to protect the reputation of an artist they represent by bidding up prices at auctions.

The gallery market is heavily fragmented, and, like the artists they represent, a tiny fraction of galleries account for much of the total turnover. For our purposes, I have divided art galleries into four categories, followed by their descriptions:

- **Alpha: 4**
- **Beta: 500**
- **Gamma: 4,000**
- **Delta: 15,480**

GALLERY BREAKDOWN

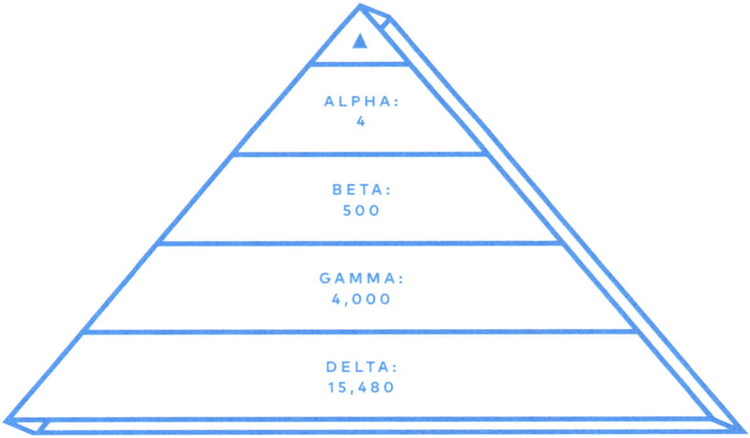

SOURCE: RESCH, 2011, PHD THESIS

Alpha

Alpha galleries are superstar galleries with superstar clients. They have major global brand awareness and usually have galleries in several cities around the world. They are key players on the secondary market and participate in the top art fairs, such as Art Basel and Frieze, where they are given prime booths. These galleries constitute the Holy Land. There are only four alpha galleries: Gagosian, David Zwirner, Pace, and Hauser & Wirth. Their revenue is around the $1 billion mark.

Beta

Beta galleries have nationwide brand awareness but less global recognition. They too have galleries in more than one location and take the remaining spots at the top art fairs, after the alpha galleries have been accommodated in the prime spots. Beta galleries tend to represent mature and emerging artists; any superstar artists are often poached, or may be co-represented, by alpha galleries. Examples include Ropac, Perrotin, Sprüth Magers, and Lehmann Maupin. Their revenue is between $50 million and $250 million, making the revenue gap between alpha and beta galleries an eye-watering three-quarters of a billion dollars. This is how far the four alpha galleries are removed from the rest (with the exception of Ropac and White Cube whose revenue is in between Alpha and Beta level).

There are several ways to collect, from blindly following advice on what to buy to trusting your gut and the emotions that art creates in you. I go with the second one! Bruno Bolfo, Collector

Gamma

Gamma galleries have little brand awareness and participate in second-tier art fairs, such as Liste Basel, NADA, Aqua Art Fair, Untitled, and Expo Chicago. These galleries represent high-street and vanity artists. Their collector base is small, and no strong ties with important museums exist. Their annual revenue is between $500,000 and $5 million. Again, the revenue gap between beta and gamma galleries makes any movement between categories highly unlikely.

Delta

Delta galleries have little to no brand awareness and do not participate in art fairs unless they are small and local—Art Karlsruhe, perhaps, or Art Zurich, or the Affordable Art Fair. They represent only passion and vanity artists. Their revenue is between $10,000 and $500,000.

6.2 Key Gallerists

Gallerists, as we have repeatedly emphasized, are the gatekeepers to the art world; their near-outright control is based on the dependence of artists and museums on them to finance their activities. There are twenty thousand gallerists, and the landscape is continuously changing, as most galleries don't stick around for too long. Here are five dealers to know (all from the alpha and beta categories):

Larry Gagosian of Gagosian

Larry Gagosian, perhaps the biggest name in the gallery game, is the founder and owner of the Gagosian gallery empire. Based in New York, Gagosian has nineteen locations worldwide and a revenue of around $1 billion. Gagosian represents mostly superstars, such as Damien Hirst and Georg Baselitz, and the estates of artists such as Picasso, Warhol, and Giacometti. Born in 1945, he is the Elon Musk of the art world, and a natural salesman. The art world now watches to see if a successor to his imperium will emerge.

David Zwirner of David Zwirner

While Gagosian may be the biggest name, David Zwirner is considered one of the most influential people in the art world (according to Power 100, an annual ranking by *ArtReview*). His gallery has eight locations from New York to London to Hong Kong, and he too records revenues of around $1 billion. Zwirner represents more than sixty artists and estates, including Franz West, Yayoi Kusama, and Jason Rhoades. Born in 1964 in Germany to a gallerist father, Zwirner is considered the king in waiting for when Gagosian steps down.

Collect art based on what speaks to you and inspires you, instead of seeing it as an investment.

LeRoy Bennett, Collector

Manuela Hauser and Iwan Wirth of Hauser & Wirth

The *ArtReview* Power 100 list also frequently names Manuela Hauser and Iwan Wirth in their top ten. Born into the art world as the daughter of collector Ursula Hauser, Manuela Hauser married Iwan Wirth, and together they founded their gallery in 1992. Hauser & Wirth now has an impressive seventeen locations across the globe, including in New York, London, Los Angeles, and Hong Kong, with an estimated revenue of around $800 million to $1 billion. They represent artists including Mark Bradford and Amy Sherald, along with some artist estates. The Swiss couple is known for their impressive, museum-like gallery spaces, usually designed by world-famous architects.

Try to surround yourself with intellectually smart and curious people. Artists, collectors, curators: get out there and be curious with people you share a passion with.

Oleg Guerrand-Hermès, Collector

Marc Glimcher of Pace Gallery

Pace Gallery was founded by Arne Glimcher in 1960 and is now run by his son, Marc Glimcher. Pace has seven locations worldwide (New York, London, Hong Kong, Palo Alto, Geneva, Seoul, and Palm Beach) and a revenue of around $1 billion. They represent artists and artist estates including Christo and Willem de Kooning. The gallery has also embarked on numerous initiatives, such as Superblue, the art experience in Miami, and Pace Ventures, which explores combinations of art and technology. Pace is very much a Glimcher family affair, with family members involved in all of the day-to-day operations in the gallery, on top of a team of more than two hundred employees.

Fall in love time and time again with work that moves you. If you select well, the work will rise in value simply because it improved the quality of your life.

Jessica Goldman Srebnick, Collector

Jeffrey Deitch of Deitch Projects

Jeffrey Deitch, born in 1950, is a legendary American art dealer and curator, who opened his first gallery in 1972. Deitch has an MBA from Harvard Business School, worked for some time as a banker, and invented what is now known as Art Banking. He was also, from 2010 until his resignation in 2013, director of the Museum of Contemporary Art, Los Angeles. Deitch has two gallery locations—one in SoHo, New York City, and one in Los Angeles. While his gallery's revenue is not in the billion-dollar range, and thus would classify as a beta gallery, Deitch is a key influencer and one of the most enduring gallerists in the world.

Other beta galleries to know:

- **Almine Rech (Paris, Brussels, London, New York, Shanghai)**
- **Blum & Poe (Los Angeles, New York)**
- **David Kordansky (Los Angeles, New York)**
- **Lévy Gorvy Dayan (New York)**
- **Marian Goodman (New York, Paris, London)**
- **Max Hetzler (Berlin, Paris, London, Marfa)**
- **Perrotin (New York, Los Angeles, Dubai, Paris, Hong Kong, Seoul, Tokyo, Shanghai)**
- **Sadie Coles HQ (London)**
- **Sprüth Magers (Berlin, New York, London, Los Angeles)**
- **Victoria Miro (London, Venice)**

6.3 Gallery Data

6·3·1 Geographical Distribution

The international gallery market for fine art comprises roughly 20,000 galleries across 124 countries and around 3,500 cities. The largest markets by number of galleries are the US (34%), Germany (12%), and the UK (10%). Combined, the three countries account for more than 50% of the total market, with slightly more than 10,000 galleries. In the Asian corner of the market, Japan accounts for 2%, followed by China (1%). In terms of place, Europe and the US are the two most important locations for the art market, housing

83% of all galleries worldwide. Asia is still a relatively minor player, with 9% of all galleries, which is surprising given that the Asian art market's value, meaning the turnover in the region, ranks among the top three in the world.

Choose works of art the way you choose your friends—they keep you company, so decide what matters most to you and stick to the plan!

Heidi Zuckerman, Curator

There is no real deviation from country data in terms of geographical significance when viewed by city. New York tops the table with 6% of total gallery distribution, followed by London with 5% and Berlin with 4%, accounting for 15% of total art-gallery distribution. The remaining enterprises are distributed among 3,530 cities, the most significant of which are Paris (3%), Los Angeles (3%), Chicago (2%), and San Francisco (2%).

6·3·2
Revenue and Profit, Costs

Art-gallery revenue in all its major markets is low, with 55% of all galleries in the US, UK, and Germany producing revenues below $200,000 a year. Revenue figures, moreover, are traditionally quoted before the usual fifty-fifty commission split is applied—the gallery retains only half of that revenue, passing the remainder over to the artist. At the top end, a few galleries do make money, with 16% achieving revenues of more than $1 million and 7% exceeding $5 million. This is in line with our classification into alpha, beta, gamma, and delta galleries; the vast majority of gamma and delta galleries show revenues of considerably less than $5 million.

Build a good network and educate yourself—find your aesthetic and look for good representations of the artist you like. Don't be afraid to buy.

John Marquez, Collector

A breakdown by country shows profit to be weighted heavily toward a small number of galleries, with only 26%

clearing more than $1 million in revenue. Low revenue doesn't necessarily mean slender profit, but in the gallery world, all too often it does. Of all galleries, 30% operate in the red, and only 18% make a healthy profit margin of more than 20%.[1] To put it another way, at the top end (alpha and beta galleries), a few galleries have worked out how to run a highly lucrative gallery space, but at the lower end (beta and gamma galleries), there is a sea of galleries that produce little profit—or none at all.

Every art piece I have acquired opened up so many worlds for me—new visions, perspectives, philosophies, and knowledge. You will gain immeasurably more than you bargained for.

Teo Yang, Collector

Why are galleries so unprofitable? Most galleries have the same four highest costs: rent (gallery space and warehouse), salaries, art fairs (minus transportation), and transportation. Rent is the top expense, since most galleries are located in premium locations in cities. They are closed three or four months of the year, making those spaces deadweight economically for up to a third of the year.

Another reason for poor profit numbers lies in the product mix. The average gallery represents thirty-three artists, but a significant proportion of their sales may well come from just one leading artist, who is often responsible for 45% of sales at smaller galleries (those with an annual turnover of less than $1 million) and 29% of sales at bigger galleries (an annual turnover of more than $10 million). Leading artists subsidize all other artists, and if they get poached by a larger gallery—which frequently happens, since contracts don't exist—the gallery is left with nothing.

Buy with your heart and your eyes, not your ears.

Michael Chutko, Collector

Given the tough market conditions, a high failure rate among galleries is inevitable. In general, galleries do not

[1] Profit margin is the net income divided by revenue. It measures how much out of every dollar of revenue a company actually keeps in earnings. Profit margin is very useful when comparing companies in a similar industry. Profit margin is displayed as a percentage; a 20% profit margin, for example, means the company has a net income of twenty cents for each dollar of sales.

GALLERY PROFITS

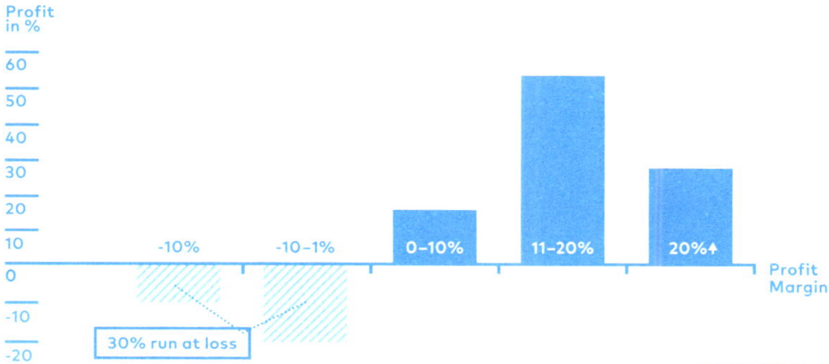

SOURCE: RESCH, 2016

have long histories. Galleries simply cannot replicate the historical sustainability of auction houses. Even powerhouses such as Gagosian have no clear succession plan, unlike the enduring names of Christie's or Sotheby's. Since 2020 galleries have opened and others have closed in almost identical numbers. The more optimistic side of this, however, is that while fewer galleries are opening (there has been an 86% decline in openings over the past decade), the rate of closure is slowing alongside it, meaning that galleries are surviving longer.

6·3·3
Galleries and Art Fairs

Art fairs, for galleries, are the equivalent of an international presence, giving gallerists a window of a few days to court collectors from around the world. The number of art fairs has shot up over the last decade, mostly because galleries want to expand and show artists internationally. Large turnouts at gallery openings may look impressive, but don't be fooled: openings are populated mostly by visitors rather than buyers. Even taking art fairs into account, galleries—small or large—have on average seventy buyers. The difference is that alpha and beta galleries have buyers with deeper pockets who purchase at higher prices and more frequently.

Today there are nearly three hundred art fairs around the world. Around half of the global gallery estate does not take part in art fairs, but among the half that does, most show at one to three per year. A notable 14% attend four or more fairs. They have good reason to invest in attendance: current figures show that 45% of total sales come from deals made at art fairs (up from 30% in 2010).

6.4 Select the Right Gallery

The gallery data above shows how broadly revenue and profits of galleries differ. Only a few make realistic profits, while most are struggling. Selecting the right gallery matters because, quite simply, a successful gallery can boost the career of the artist you buy, an important factor whether you have invested in them as a potential rising asset or you simply want to see them thrive. There are twenty thousand galleries, so finding the one that fits you is not easy. The run-through of art-market economics above may not seem directly relevant at this moment, but an understanding of the whole market environment will put you on a surer footing as you identify the gallery you are looking for.

Collect the unexpected. A unique voice in a collection is exciting and invariably provides deeper moments for exploration. Collecting a checklist is shopping; engaging with art and artists from broader contexts is ambitious and community building.
Claire Breukel, Curator

I developed a two-step approach to help you classify any gallery:

6·4·1

Step 1: Visit the Website

In a radical and counterintuitive reversal of the advice you might expect regarding websites and personal visits, an initial review of your gallery's website is essential. Most galleries have an identical look and feel physically, which completely robs them of any clue as to their classification: heavy doors, sterile rooms with white walls, various intense lights shining on the artworks, great locations, and completely empty, apart from you and a bored assistant sitting at the front desk. Even now, after having been to so many galleries, I can't classify them solely from the way they look.

Don't buy it. Wait and get your eye mileage in before starting to acquire. Your taste changes after you have done your homework. Vajra Kingsley, Curator

6·4·2

Step 2: Apply Our Criteria

Once you are on their website, apply our criteria.
As a reminder, here are the criteria to classify galleries:

- **Representation: Which type of artists does the gallery represent? Superstars, mature/emerging, main-street, vanity, passion artists?**

This is the gold-standard method for classification, as, above all else, you can identify a gallery by the artists it shows. A superstar artist doesn't show in a beta gallery, nor a vanity artist in an alpha. I gave you the tools to classify artists. Once you have classified either the gallery or the artist, your classification of both is established. A gallery's website always shows the list of artists they represent. A caveat: there is a crucial difference between the artists they represent and those they have worked with. "Artists worked with" refers to artists who the gallery has maybe included in a group show, or perhaps the gallerist sold a work of theirs on the secondary market. Often, gamma or even delta galleries include works by superstar artists in their group shows, as they hope that their vanity/passion artists will benefit from a brand spillover. Anyone who owns a work by a superstar artist can include it in their show. You're looking for the list that clearly says, "Artists represented by the gallery."

▸ **Art fairs: What type of art fairs does the gallery participate at?**

A fast way to identify the classification of any gallery, if you don't recognize the classification of the artists they're showing, is to look at the fairs they attend. Gallery websites often have a page for art fairs, or you may find the information on an exhibitions page. Participation at Art Basel, Frieze, or TEFAF indicates an alpha or beta gallery; Art Miami, Art Fair Cologne, Art Zurich, and Discover Art Fair Frankfurt, among others, would suggest a gamma gallery. (We will talk about art fairs, including the clues offered about gallery classification by booth location, in more detail in a later chapter.)

Every piece of art you acquire should be a source of joy and pride, regardless of value. Let each piece express who you are. Mouna Atassi, Collector

▸ **Brand recognition: How well-known is the brand? How many Instagram followers does the gallery have? Who's written about it in the press? How long has it been in business?**

Brands in the art world are generally known only within the art world and not beyond. Art Basel, Sotheby's, and MoMA are big brands known to a larger audience, but you may not have heard of Pace Gallery or David Zwirner before reading this book. Galleries have little to no brand recognition in the mainstream. One proxy for identifying the brand value of a gallery is their Instagram following. The bigger galleries have been successful in getting a large number of followers, although several gamma and delta galleries have done some really good social media work to attract followers as well. Even more

Look in the other direction and avoid following trends or imposing unnecessary limitations. Alexander Adler, Advisor

important, I think, is who follows these accounts. If I see art-world people who I trust following an account, I take it as a tip that this gallery might be one to watch.

Let's apply this to a few galleries:

6·4·3
Applying It in Practice

Alpha: Gagosian

▸ **Representation:** Gagosian represents the world's leading artists. You need only glance at the list of artists they work with and you will immediately recognize superstar artists both past and present, such as Hirst, Giacometti, Picasso, and Warhol.

▸ **Art fairs:** Gagosian participates at the world's leading fairs, including Art Basel, Frieze, and TEFAF.

▸ **Brand recognition:** You will see that Gagosian has a large Instagram following, which includes many of the art world's most influential people, together with an assortment of celebrities.

Beta: David Nolan Gallery

▸ **Representation:** David Nolan Gallery, based in New York, is not a household name like Gagosian, even among collectors. A quick review of their website and the artists they represent will not help either. You probably won't recognize any names there: no Warhols or Picassos.

▸ **Art fairs:** Like Gagosian, Nolan participates at the key art fairs, such as Art Basel in Basel or Frieze Art Fair. The lack of the superstar artists excludes him from alpha status, but his presence at the most important art fairs confirms Nolan's position in the beta tier. The artists he represents will be in the mature/emerging category, with corresponding price points of around $50,000 to $1 million.

▸ **Brand recognition:** The brand's recognition is solid but on a lower level than Gagosian. Even ten thousand followers on Instagram gives Nolan less than 10% of Gagosian's reach.

Gamma: Galerie von Stechow

‣ **Representation:** If you go through their list of artists, you will almost certainly not recognize any names. To get a better sense of the classification, a look at the art fairs will help.

‣ **Art fairs:** The gallery actively participates at art fairs, such as Art Miami, Art Fair Cologne, Art Zurich, Discover Art Fair Frankfurt, and others. These are not alpha or beta art fairs but gamma fairs, placing the gallery in the corresponding tier.

‣ **Brand recognition:** Their brand recognition is lower than Nolan's, with fewer than five thousand followers on Instagram.

Delta: Blue Print Gallery

‣ **Representation:** If you go through their list, you will see a lot of artists. I really like their work, but you'll notice that none are of superstar or mature/emerging classification. Most are vanity artists.

‣ **Art fairs:** Art-fair participation is nonexistent, or very limited. I can only find the Southampton Art Fair on their website, which is a small and regional fair in the Hamptons.

‣ **Brand recognition:** Their brand recognition is strong on Instagram, with more than eighty thousand followers. The gallery seems to be a side enterprise to a well-known interior-design store in Dallas.

6·4·4
Summary

It is important to establish the classification of a gallery, as this is a key factor in assessing the value—not necessarily the investment value but the actual price you should be paying—for the artist's work you are buying. To reiterate, galleries and artists are closely linked: a superstar artist shows in an alpha gallery, while a beta gallery shows mature/emerging artists. If you've set your heart on a particular work in a high price bracket, you can buy with more confidence if you know that you are buying a work of art from an artist with

Follow your eye.
Adam Chinn, Advisor

some degree of reputation and exposure, from a gallery that has a track record of supporting their career.

And to retread ground that we've already covered: there is no bad art, there are no bad artists, and there are no bad galleries. The tier in which a gallery belongs does not mean that a piece you want to buy is without merit or of lesser merit—nor does it mean that it won't bring you joy and excitement, as art should. I personally buy from delta galleries. It gives me great pleasure to find delta artists and buy from delta galleries—not only am I getting great art but I'm also supporting a community. I take what I call responsible buying very seriously—the idea of not only buying as an investment but also as a philanthropic act. Nonetheless, when I buy from delta galleries, it is very important that the price is adjusted to their classification. I would never buy a piece for $20,000 from a delta gallery. To prevent you from making that mistake, I wrote this book.

Don't settle for average. Be very selective and aim to get the best of the artists you want to buy. Even if it means waiting and paying more, it pays off.

Alexandre Errera, Advisor

Be close to knowledgeable people in the art world, but follow your instinct and follow your love. Educate your eye with seeing quality and take risks. Do not wait too long when you are interested in something.

Désiré Feuerle, Collector

6·4·5

Dos and Don'ts

Dos

- **Visit the website before you do anything else to identify the art fairs where the gallery is showing.**
- **Look out for superstar artists or familiar names to get an immediate indication of classification.**
- **If you can't find the list of art fairs but you see some bigger artist names, ask if the gallery shows at Art Basel, Frieze, or TEFAF—the three alpha fairs.**

Don'ts

▸ Don't be scared to ask who else is represented by the gallery. The gallerist will always pull out the biggest names.
▸ Don't be scared to ask for the price.
▸ Don't be misled by the gallery's location or appearance. In most cases, they all look the same, from alpha down to delta.
▸ Don't be surprised when you find Picasso or Warhol or Koons listed on a delta website. They might list it to show that they have access to these works or have sold a work by them in the past. Often they list them under "Artists worked with." It's a marketing technique galleries use to show relevance.
▸ Don't fall into the misconception that gamma or delta galleries show bad artists. There are no bad artists. There are artists you like and artists you don't like.

6.5 Buying through Galleries

Assuming you have found your gallery and artist, we are going to run through the process of purchasing from a gallery.

6·5·1 Step 1: Requesting the Price

One of the more daunting aspects of galleries for newcomers is the fact that there are no prices on display. You need to request them. What then follows is what I call the beauty contest. A gallery assistant, usually an unpaid or underpaid intern, will possibly hand you the price list but may also ask for your name. She will then go behind the scenes and find the owner of the gallery, who will then appear and give you the price, going on to ask about your collection, what you are interested in, who you are, and so on.

Why is it so difficult to find out the price? I have no idea. I think it's useless and stops people from buying art. In all my books, talks, and consulting activities, I have advised galleries against this practice. But many galleries are still doing it and justifying it by saying that they "want to engage in a dialogue" if someone requests a price. I think it's an old-school sales technique that does more harm than good.

There is this myth of a collector with "a good eye," a person born with good taste and who makes great choices. This fails to acknowledge the fact that collecting art is a discipline, an exercise in curiosity and risk-taking. Jam Acuzar, Collector

Since you are likely to have to endure the beauty contest, however, here are my thoughts. In conversation with the gallerist, you can and should be very open about your background. If it's your first piece, just say so. And don't try to overstate your collection. The art world is very small, so if you have a big collection, people will know you, and if you don't, it will take the gallerist two phone calls to find out that you were exaggerating. So just be honest about your interest and your status as a collector.

As a slight aside to the gallery buying process, if you found an artist on Instagram, don't spend time researching the gallery. Often, gallery websites are outdated and list artists they no longer show. Simply reach out to the artist and ask about the price of the work. If the artist is not bound to a gallery and sells directly, she will tell you the price. If the artist is represented by a gallery, then she will refer incoming inquiries via Instagram to the right gallery. In other words, it's absolutely fine to connect with an artist via Instagram if you found them online and take it from there, but if you found the artist in the gallery, then contact the gallerist directly. If you see an artist in a show, then in almost all cases the artist will refer you to the gallery.

Follow your heart, not a hedge fund. And leave your wallet at home until you determine what you love. Ron Pizzuti, Collector

Artists generally don't circumvent their galleries, and particularly not when shows are on.

6·5·2
Step 2: Evaluating the Price

You have decided that you like the work, and the gallerist has given you the price. Frequently, pricing in the art world is neither logical nor rational, and if you are new to the art world, there is little or no sense of relative value as there might be in more familiar markets like fashion or luxury cars. All this makes it a challenge to determine if an artwork's price is too high.

A number of factors can affect the price:

- **Materials used to make the work and other related expenses**
- **Time spent on the production**
- **Size**
- **Motive**
- **Quality (i.e., Is this a highly finished piece or more of a draft?)**
- **Condition**
- **Is it an edition, and if so, how many editions are there?**

These factors have an understandable connection to price that is certainly reflected in what you will pay, but as you now know from the chapter above discussing my research into five hundred thousand artists, these factors are incidental to the absolutely no. 1 factor: the gallery where the artist is shown. Moving beyond that, however, the Artist Framework in the earlier chapter helps you to establish if the gallery is asking for a fair price. I have taken a similar logic in the Budget Framework in the following graphic, since financial limitations (budgets) drive the most common questions I hear: "What can I get for $3,000?" and "How can I get an investment piece for $3,000?" To help you make decisions with limited spending power, review the Budget Framework.

As you can see on page 140, the first column includes your budget options. The following two columns match the budget to the artist and gallery categories, followed by two columns for prices and finally a column for investment potential. As you'd expect, investment potential is low for more than 80% of all artists, medium for mature/emerging artists, and high for superstar artists.

In practice, if you are on a budget of $3,000, you will probably end up buying from a vanity or passion artist. Your best tactic would be to buy directly from the artist, perhaps from an artist platform such as saatchiart.com, where artists can upload their works, or you could buy from delta galleries, which you can find at delta art fairs. This framework also prevents you from overpaying. If you are buying from a delta gallery or a passion artist but the price tag is $30,000, you should be cautious, as it's almost certainly overpriced.

A personal narrative makes it easier to identify artists that will stir you emotionally. It also helps focus the mind at art fairs, galleries, and auction previews, which are always chockablock with too much art.
Doug Woodham, Advisor

Of course, these tables are simplifications, and any rules you might infer from them are not set in stone, as artist prices vary even within the same classification. A superstar artist such as Gerhard Richter has a different average price point than superstar artist Christopher Wool, and a mature artist such as Marilyn Minter has a lower price than mature artist Robert Longo. An edition of superstar artist Damien Hirst starts at a much lower price point than $500,000, and you can also buy it from a gamma gallery. The overall direction and systematic setup of the framework, however, should serve as a starting point and give you a useful benchmark to navigate prices in the market.

Figure out which artist you most want to own a work by. Then look everywhere to see if there is one work good enough that you can also afford—if not, move to the next. Josh Baer, Advisor

BUDGET FRAMEWORK

BUDGET per artwork	ARTISTS	GALLERIES	PRICE RANGE small works large works	PRICE POINT large unique work	INVESTMENT POTENTIAL
$500,000	SUPERSTAR	ALPHA	$500k and up	$2M	HIGH
$50,000	MATURE/ EMERGING	BETA	$50k–$1M	$100k	MEDIUM
$20,000	HIGH-STREET	GAMMA	$5–$50k	$15k	LOW
$10,000	VANITY	DELTA	$1–$50k	$7k	LOW
$5,000	PASSION		$1–$10k	$3k	LOW

I would also encourage you to continue asking questions if a price doesn't make sense to you. There might be reasons why the price is high or low. Gallerists will always be happy to answer questions and explain, and if you are dealing with an artist who has a history on the secondary market, you can press for information from a more informed perspective, armed with historic trading prices.

6·5·3
Step 3: Make an Offer

Once you have decided that the price the gallery is asking for is within your budget and fair, you will need to make an offer. This can introduce other difficulties because not every artwork that you see is for sale. Sometimes it's already taken, reserved, or the gallerist doesn't want to sell it to you. I'm going to run through some of the typical obstacles that can arise when making an offer.

Access to Artists

Access to superstar artists is rare. Demand exceeds supply, as collectors are all aware of the investment potential of both superstars and some mature/emerging artists who have been expertly hyped and are currently in vogue. (This certainly doesn't apply to any other artist classifications from our framework.) The dealer's job is to select where the work ends up, a decision based on three key factors.

First of all, she wants to place the work in the hands of eminent collectors and institutions. This helps to build up and preserve the reputation of the in-demand artist. Inclusion in a big collection helps to extend the reach of the artist and increases her credibility. Collectors will talk positively about it, introduce the artist to curators of museums, and showcase the artist to other gallerists and collectors. Essentially, they work as unpaid ambassadors to the artists. Any gallerist representing an artist will want the work to end up with such powerful influencers.

Ask yourself: Why do you want to collect? If you really love art, enjoy the ride. If you want to make money, steer clear.
Felix Krämer, Museum Director

Second, with artists who are in demand, gallerists can sell to only a handful of collectors—and in all likelihood to a known collector who has built up a loyalty with the gallerist. In order to keep her most long-standing clients, she will sell to them rather than using them as inducements to the newest buyer to walk through the door.

Third, gallerists are wary of speculators, as they want to limit the risk of losing control of the artist's market. A speculator might buy a work and then flip it, passing it on to an auction house for a quick profit. To avoid the loss of control over pricing that can come with auctions—where works can also sell for below the gallery price, harming its reputation—the representatives of in-demand artists have started to include terms in their invoices that prevent buyers from reselling the works within the next five years.

Don't be afraid to "overpay" for the very best by an artist. "Overpaying" is sometimes the only way to pry something phenomenal out, but then you end up with something that will typically be more valuable in the long run. But do it assiduously.
Bernie Lagrange, Advisor

Blacklist

Access problems also include blacklists, something I sincerely hope you will neither invite nor experience. Blacklists identify collectors who engage in practices that the gallerist or artist consider a violation of their standards. For example, flippers get blacklisted—even if the resale happens privately and not at a public auction. The art world is very small, and dealers constantly speak with each other. So if you are interested in making a lot of money by flipping works, be assured that this strategy won't last long, as you will be blocked from buying eventually.

Bargaining Power

Hurdles to access based on personal credibility and getting blacklisted because of flipping might sound interesting and make good headline stories and lawsuits, but these cases are very rare, cropping up in only a very few cases for superstars or mature/emerging artists who are in particularly high demand. With almost all other artists, certainly all mainstreet, vanity, and passion artists, supply exceeds demand almost without exception. Frankly, any gallerist is thrilled just to make a sale because of the pitiful economics at the lower end of the art market. Any sense of urgency and scarcity when you are hesitating over a work in a gamma gallery is almost guaranteed to be a sales strategy rather than fact. Your bargaining power in a gallery is extremely high, and you should feel empowered to exercise it.

Collect what speaks to you, what pulls you, and what tugs at your heart. Collect what you love, and you will enjoy having it in your home for a long time.
Tariku Shiferaw, Artist

Negotiation Strategies

If you are negotiating to overcome a resistant gallerist hesitant to sell to a new buyer, there are a couple of ideas that might convince a gallerist to sell you a work:

- **Offering to buy the work of one other artist in the gallery's program who is currently not high in demand is a common sweetener when buying the work of a hot artist. It shows**

your commitment to the gallery, and the gallerist can sell something for an underappreciated or under-exposed artist.

- **Offering to buy two works—one to donate to a museum—is common and beneficial for all parties, though it is not without its own obstacles. The gallerist wins, as she can donate a work to a museum and strengthen her ties with it. The artist benefits as she gets money for both works and is included in a museum collection. The museum gets a good work free of charge and expands its museum collection. And the collector not only gets his own work but also gets his name on the wall at a museum, plus a tax write-off. What sounds like a win for all parties, however, is difficult to actually put into practice. Legal requirements for tax-write-off benefits are strict, including demands that the donation be educational and the artwork is put on display, as well as prohibitions on donating an artwork immediately after purchase and a requirement of a price evaluation of the work approved by the museum. Even finding a museum to accept a work is harder than you think. Museums have become reluctant to add works to their collection, as every work requires insurance, storage space, and attention. Museums may only want to add major works, and the works that the gallerist has available may not appeal to the museum curator, even if they already have other works by the same artist.**

For all other artists, however—and, practically speaking, this means 99.9% of all artworks you will see—you can negotiate the price. It's common practice. Here are some strategies you can employ to get a good deal:

- **Cash is king. Offer it.**
- **Offer to pay immediately, today.**
- **Confirm that you won't sell the work.**
- **Ask the dealer to pay for shipping so you don't have to. It's generally understood that shipping is paid for by the buyer, so if you can get it thrown in, it's effectively a discount.**
- **If you buy at an art fair and the dealer is from a different country, come back on the last day. The dealer might accept**

a lower offer to avoid transportation costs back to her country.
▸ Build up a relationship and don't be afraid to show authentic interest. While you shouldn't lose your head over money, this is also not a time for playing it cool about the piece. Gallerists are passionate about the artists they are selling. They want to find a great home for them. So show genuine interest and excitement about the art.

In general, asking for a 20% discount is neither unethical nor bad manners, if you pay immediately. Nor, however, should you take it personally if you can't seal the deal at the offer price you make. Gallerists are within their rights to say no. There may be good reasons why they need to stick to full price, but they may well make a counteroffer. If you want to establish an ongoing relationship with the gallerist, however, you should only enter negotiations with the gallerist for works that you can afford at full price. A gallerist will soon tire of a client who persistently attempts to secure work below price because they don't quite have the funds to get what they want.

6·5·4
Step 4: After the Sale

Once you have agreed on a price and deal terms, there are a few logistics to discuss.

Invoice

The dealer will send you an invoice. This often serves as a document of authenticity to prove that the artwork is real and created by this artist. The invoice should always include the name of the artist, title, year, medium, size, and edition number, plus a small image of the work.

Certificate of Authenticity

If the invoice doesn't contain these details, ask for a certificate of authenticity, which includes the information above, plus the signature of the artist. It's not standard practice to receive this, but you can ask for it.

Transportation

The dealer never pays for transportation or hanging but will share the details of her preferred partner. International shipping can be costly and usually takes time. It goes without saying that you may want to think twice before committing to the process of shipping fragile works overseas. Shipping paintings overseas can be easier if they are taken out of the frame and rolled in a tube. Framing costs once you get them home can be cheaper than shipping them framed.

Timing

Even once you have bought the work, if it's in a show, it stays on view until the show's closing date, possibly a period of some weeks. The wait is normally shorter if you buy at art fairs, particularly if a fair is in your city, as the work can be left by the dealer when she packs up. If neither you nor the dealer lives in the city where the fair was held, you will need to discuss when the work can be picked up by your shipping company.

> **Don't be afraid of artists and works you didn't know yet or that you've never heard of, or of being alone in wanting to collect!**
> Chris Dercon, Museum Director

Loan

The dealer might ask if you would agree to delay delivery to allow it to be temporarily hung at a museum or another gallery's exhibition before it's delivered to you. Always agree to this. If your work is shown in a museum or another gallery show or is part of a catalogue, it lends extra credibility to the work. You can then speak of provenance, which—depending on the institution—can add extra value.

6·5·5
Dos and Don'ts

Dos

▸ **Be honest when you introduce yourself to a gallerist. They will find out if your collection is not as big as you said.**

▸ **Use the Budget Framework when evaluating the price. It helps you spot overpriced or underpriced artists.**

- **If the artist is in demand, offer to buy two or donate one to a museum.**
- **Always ask for an invoice that includes the key elements, such as name, photo of the work, etc. This acts as a certificate of authenticity.**
- **Ask for a discount. Galleries often give discounts of up to 20% if you pay the same day.**

Don'ts

- **Don't be scared to request prices when in a gallery.**
- **Don't expect a discount if the artist is in demand.**
- **Don't expect that you can ever sell your artwork again. Most don't have any resale value.**

6.6 Selling through Galleries

All my caveats that most work can't be resold notwithstanding, I do here address the possibility that, a few years later, you may want to sell your artwork because it's too big, too small, or you don't like it anymore. There are a few steps to consider when selling through a dealer:

6·6·1
Step 1: Check if There Is Demand

You may hear with excitement that your artist's prices have gone up and the dealer is now selling them for more, leading to the conclusion that your asset has appreciated. Sadly, in most cases, prices in galleries go up purely because the artist and the gallerist decide to raise them for reasons that have nothing to do with increased demand or other rational economics. Unless your artist has turned into a superstar or mature/emerging artist and is now represented by an alpha or beta gallery, you will be highly unlikely to resell her work.

A good indicator for the likelihood of a resale is to check any auction results for this artist. If there are no auction results, there is probably no demand. If there is a recent sale history showing sale prices well above your own work, you should reach out to your gallerist first (before any other option) and ask her if she is interested in buying it back or might have a buyer for it. If an artist is in demand, gallerists are often approached by potential buyers, and she may well have a buyer lined up already. Remember, access to sought-after artists is one of the key difficulties in buying their work. So offering one to your gallerist first will be considered a proof of trust. Even if the gallerist doesn't buy it back, or can't broker a deal, she will appreciate the approach.

Collect because you enjoy what an art piece brings into your life inherently in its existence, not monetarily in its "worth."
Sophia Cohen, Gallerist

6·6·2
Step 2: Pricing Your Artwork

Finding a price for an artwork is an art, not a science. There are four ways to determine what the right price might be:

- **Go with your original buying price. If you are able to recover the price you initially paid, that's a win.**
- **Look at the most recent prices in galleries and auctions for this artist and cross-check against works of this size and medium. Just be aware that auction prices can be artificially inflated or depressed relative to gallery prices for all kinds of reasons that don't necessarily reflect the selling potential of the artist.**
- **Ask for an estimate by an auction house. If you see work by the artist offered at a particular auction house, send a photo of your work to their art valuer and ask for an estimate (and I write more about selling through auction in a later chapter). Auction house estimates are free and will give you a good starting point for the negotiation with the gallerist.**

- **Approach an appraiser. The Appraisers Association of America (AAA) might be a reliable resource for finding qualified appraisers in specialized areas. These appraisals, however, cost money (amounts can vary) and take several weeks. In general, I would advise against this, unless your work is from an emerging/mature or superstar artist.**

6·6·3
Step 3: Sign a Consignment Agreement

In the rare case that the gallerist sees an opportunity to sell your work, she will probably not buy the work directly from you but offer the work on your behalf to her client, taking a commission. In this event, you will need to define the terms in a consignment agreement.

Important points in a consignment agreement are:

- **Price: What is the lowest price the gallerist can offer the work for?**
- **Commission: Usually gallerists will get 20–25% of the sales value. Sometimes gallerists like to negotiate a fixed amount with the owner, one that they are comfortable they can achieve. The rest of the proceeds—an amount typically unknown to the collector—will then go to the gallerist. I always prefer the percentage model because it makes the sales process more transparent.**
- **Timeline: How long does the gallerist have the exclusive right to sell the work? Selling through a gallerist often takes time. They might include the work in an upcoming group show or take it to an art fair. A sale won't happen overnight and often takes much more time than you would imagine.**
- **Expenses: Who covers shipping, photography, and marketing? If the work is going from you to a gallery, then the gallerist will often pay shipping; if the work is sold, the new buyer pays for shipping. But dealers like to**

> Collecting art is personal. If it is a journey that you want to embark on, start by figuring out your "why." It will help to define your collection.
>
> Ato & Tonya Wright, Collectors

deduct cost of shipping from the sales price, and other costs like photography can add up. Make sure that all costs associated with the sale and who pays them are clearly identified.

- **Marketing: Sometimes gallerists send the work out to too many potential buyers or add too many advisors to widen their distribution channels. Dealers then consider this work "burned," meaning that the work was pitched to too many people at the same time, which confuses potential buyers and makes the work less attractive. Don't be afraid to ask, in some detail, what marketing activities your gallerist is conducting, so that you can get a feel for whether they are adopting a carefully targeted approach or can justify a broader one.**

Selling through the gallerist you purchased it from is always the preferred option. If she is no longer in business or not interested, look at other galleries representing the artist, and approach auction houses directly. Take a look at the auction house chapter to see what to consider when selling through an auction house and why it might be a preferred method for some pieces.

Think about what your goals are. Are you buying art for personal satisfaction; to reflect a particular genre or culture; to tell a story, a history, or point of view; or to build a "best-in-class" collection? There are many reasons why one collects, and those reasons may change over time. Thinking about goals helps you have focus. There is so much outstanding art in the marketplace, and few collectors have unlimited budgets, so some degree of focus is beneficial. Having said that, be open to surprises, work you encounter in a gallery or an art fair that just stops you in your tracks. Some of our most treasured artworks were delightful discoveries.

Denise B. Gardner, Collector

6·6·4
Dos and Don’ts

Dos

▸ Do your research by looking at prices from auctions and galleries for your artist.

▸ Always sign a consignment agreement.

▸ Ask the gallerist you purchased it from first, then approach other galleries that show the artist and auction houses.

Don’ts

▸ Don’t assume that a gallerist will be able to sell your work just because he sold it to you. Artworks are not cars. Most don’t have any resale value.

▸ Don’t expect money to come in tomorrow. Even if a gallerist agrees to sell your work, the process can take a lot of time.

Case Study

JEFFREY DEITCH—LEGENDARY GALLERIST AND ART-WORLD ICON

Jeffrey Deitch is considered one of the most legendary art gallerists in the world. He opened his first gallery in 1972 in Massachusetts and shortly thereafter moved to New York and became involved in the international art scene. He has an MBA from Harvard Business School and invented what is now colloquially known as "art banking." He was also, from 2010 to 2013, director of the Museum of Contemporary Art in Los Angeles. When I interviewed him, Deitch explained how he maintains his integrity and how he continues to scout artists. Deitch began building his extensive network very early on. Soon after graduating from Wesleyan in 1974, he drove down to New York to approach the best-known galleries (all of which were located in the same building at the time) for a position. The art world's Holy Land happened to be there, and he stepped right into it, working as the secretary for the John Weber Gallery. Since most of the art world was located in the immediate vicinity of the building, Deitch was acquainted with all the must-know dealers, artists, and curators within a few months, and his career flourished from there.

Despite the widening global reach of the contemporary-art phenomenon, it remains a small industry with a tight network, and Deitch's network, after so many decades in the art world, is one of the best in the business. Even now, although his seventieth birthday has passed and he is older than many working artists, he keeps close tabs on the next generation of gallerists and curators so he can figure out which newer artists are worth watching. He frequently visits young and upcoming gallerists and supports them through his contacts. There is not a corner of the art world that Deitch is not completely updated on.

His network is also invaluable to his collectors and to the established artists whose works are in such a competitive marketplace and with whom he has relationships built on strong trust. Many of Deitch's clients have had a working relationship with him for years, if not decades, and those loyal buyers get first call on the best works. He knows from experience what each client is looking for, which also serves the artist community: it is critical to Deitch that in-demand artists go to the right buyer, a point he was at pains to stress when we met in his charming office.

Visiting Deitch—"I am in my seventies, and I am still working hard!"—is an object lesson in how, even after a long career, energetic scrutiny of art-market developments, a perpetual natural curiosity about what's new, and the maintenance of a constantly ringing network keeps you as busy and as sought after as anyone else in the industry. He is also a study in the wisdom of the long game—the patient cultivation of strong and loyal ties with both collectors and artists by building trust and maintaining it through lasting relationships.

ADVICE

I advise acquiring several artworks at the beginning of the art-collecting adventure and living with them at home. The collecting process then becomes more real than theoretical. It is very good to be able to understand how actual artworks will resonate. The collector might want to continue on their original path or try another direction that might be more rewarding. I also advise connecting with art historians, curators, gallerists, and other knowledgeable people. Most of my friends in the art community enjoy sharing their insights for free.

7
Art Fairs

—Buying at Art Fairs without Getting Over-whelmed

Art fairs have become the most important distribution channel for galleries, with many making as much as 50% of their annual revenue at fairs. The roughly three hundred art fairs have a strict hierarchy, and showing at the best of them lends participating galleries an invaluable stamp of approval. Fairs will also help you, as a collector, to verify the classification of the gallery.

7.1 Overview and Classification

Art fairs have become a cornerstone in the art world, and galleries make a big slice of their annual revenue at them. Unsurprisingly, the number of fairs has increased rapidly over the last twenty years. In 2000 there were fifty-five art fairs; in 2023 they number approximately three hundred.

Collect the work you like and get to know the artist. Form authentic relationships. Buck the trends; make yourself happy, intrigued; feel!

Melissa Cowley Wolf, Curator

Geographically, they are spread out, although most are in Europe, with 51%, and the US, with 28%. Visitor numbers are also on the rise, as art fairs are no longer an industry event but a social gathering. Eighty thousand people come to Art Basel at the Convention Center in Miami every year—and that doesn't count those who never even find their way to the Convention Center, diverted by the many other fairs that spring up temporarily around the main event.

At fairs, sales are often not a direct on-the-spot transaction. Only 65% of sales happen during the fair; 15% of sales happen before the fair and 20% after, a point that will become relevant very shortly.

Fairs create their revenue via two channels. The first is renting out booths. Prices for a single, small booth at alpha art fairs are between $50,000 and $70,000. Prices at beta and gamma fairs are lower, with the Armory Show starting at $40,000 or more and local fairs at less than $10,000. These starting prices for small booths can increase threefold for a larger space. From the gallerist's point of view, the total cost for staff, shipping, transportation, and insurance can bring the cost up to $400,000 for a

I always stick to Frank Gerritz's advice about collecting: it always has to hurt a little, and he only gets angry about things he didn't buy. Gregor Hildebrandt, Artist

medium-size booth at Art Basel. The gallerist will then need to make sales totaling $800,000 just to break even, after 50% of all sales have gone to the artist. The second revenue stream for fairs is sponsorship fees. Art Basel, for example, has fifteen different partners. The most important partners are banks (e.g., UBS), art-insurance groups (e.g., AXA Art), and luxury brands (e.g., BMW).

As with everything else, the three hundred art fairs can be broken down into classifications. There are three main types, followed by their description:

- **Alpha: 3**
- **Beta: 15**
- **Gamma: 280**

ART FAIR BREAKDOWN

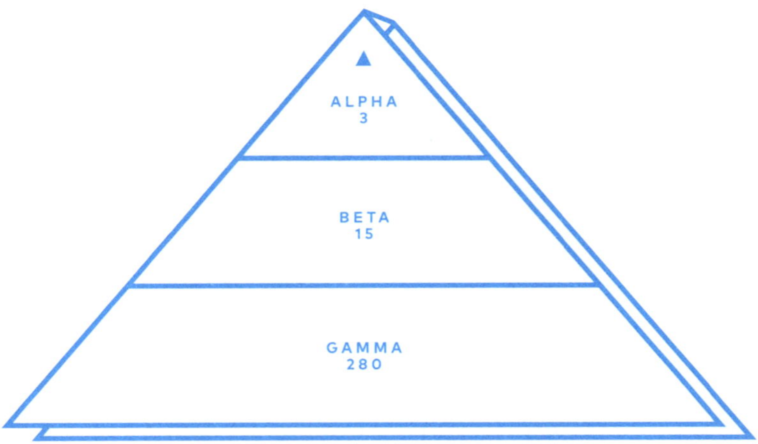

Alpha

Alpha art fairs have a global footprint with fair locations around the world. While an international footprint is important, it's the participating galleries that make a fair. At alpha fairs, you would usually expect to find the four alpha galleries exhibiting, together with a large number of beta galleries. There are only three alpha fairs: Art Basel,

Frieze, and TEFAF, with Art Basel very much first among equals. The median price for artworks at Art Basel and Frieze is around $30,000, shooting up to $100,000 at TEFAF as a reflection of its broader offering across different categories.

Beta

Beta art fairs are the extended top list. Many take place in only one location, with only a few holding an event at a second or third location. The key difference between beta and alpha fairs is that not all the alpha galleries will necessarily be there; most exhibitors are from beta and gamma galleries. Among the fifteen beta art fairs are the Armory Show and ADAA, and national art fairs such as ARCOmadrid, Art Cologne, FIAC Paris, FOG Design+Art, 1-54 Contemporary African Art Fair, and ART021 Shanghai. NADA, Liste Art Fair Basel, and Independent Art Fair showcase galleries from the network that feeds into the alpha galleries. The remainder fluctuates frequently, as the list of fifteen is highly dynamic. The median price point for artworks at beta fairs is $15,000.

Follow your heart.

George Hamilton, Collector

Gamma

Gamma fairs are regional or local art fairs, with no international presence, and only gamma or delta galleries participate. Good examples are Art International Zurich, Art Karlsruhe, and Art Düsseldorf. SCOPE Art Show and the Affordable Art Fair, both of which have several international outposts, are also part of the gamma group, with no alpha or beta participants. The list of gamma art fairs is extensive and also includes art fairs at which primarily artists are exhibiting, such as Superfine Art Fair or SPRING/BREAK Art Show. The median price point at gamma fairs is $5,000.

First, consume and explore art—look, smell, and taste it—and remember that art is a social experience. And then, when your taste has matured, start collecting, and collect what *you* love, crave, and are fascinated by!

Moran Bar-Kochva, Collector

7.2 Key Art Fairs

We'll review some art fairs so you can familiarize yourself with them, and on your next trip to Miami or New York during art-fair week, you will know which fairs to go to.

Art Basel

Art Basel is the undisputed market leader because of the quality of its exhibitors. Every alpha gallery shows there. It's a privilege and a sign of excellence for any gallery to show at Art Basel. To participate, your application needs to clear the selection committee, which is made up of gallerists. It is every gallery owner's ultimate goal to show there. Art Basel also has an international footprint. Their fair in Basel in Switzerland is considered the world's leading fair; Miami takes place in December and covers the South American market; and Hong Kong, which takes place in April, covers Asia. Roughly three hundred galleries participate at each venue. Art Basel is owned by the Swiss government (Canton of Basel) and James Murdoch, an American investor. It's named after Basel in Switzerland, where it was originally founded in 1970.

Spend some time really looking. Really looking! Not buying. Investtime in going to galleries, museums, exhibitions. Collecting is a visual and "gut" experience and a journey.

Howard E. Rachofsky, Collector

Frieze Art Fair

Frieze Art Fair takes place in London, New York, Los Angeles, and Seoul and is owned by entertainment company Endeavor. You would generally expect to find full alpha presence, or nearly so. It was originally started as a spin-off to the art magazine *Frieze*, which took advantage of their gallery contacts and created a fair to rival Art Basel. When Endeavor purchased the majority of shares in 2019, the art world expected Frieze to enlarge its footprint fast and add Endeavor's celebrity appeal to it; so far, despite the disruption of the 2020 pandemic, they have added two shows, first in Los Angeles and then in Seoul in 2022.

The European Fine Art Foundation (TEFAF)

The third and least known alpha art fair is TEFAF. It's been around for more than forty years and takes place in the small city of Maastricht in Holland. For a few years it's also been operating in New York in the Armory Building on Park Avenue. TEFAF's relevance and popularity is based on its exhibitor base, which includes not only all alpha galleries but also noncontemporary galleries. While it's rare to see a Picasso or a Monet at Art Basel, you see the real masterpieces, plus a smattering of antiquities, at TEFAF. Collectors love TEFAF because of the high-end quality of works. It's widely considered the most elegant fair in the world, attended by the biggest art collectors, who travel every year to Maastricht and recently to New York to buy pieces.

Look with your eyes, not your ears. James Fuentes, Gallerist

The Armory Show

The Armory Show is a classic beta art fair. A cornerstone of New York's cultural landscape since its founding in 1994, the Armory Show takes place annually in New York. At its 2023 edition, the top four alpha galleries didn't participate. Often, beta fair organizers even offer discounted space to these galleries but still can't persuade them to attend. I can only speculate as to why, and the reasons will vary, but they often believe that the fair won't be financially successful for them at that time, or they don't want to shift the manpower from their city locations to the fair.

Having a mission and work parameters in place not only helps to refine a collection but acts as an extension of your philanthropic efforts and goals. RF Jefferies, Curator

New Art Dealers Alliance (NADA)

NADA art fair is another example of a beta fair. It's a small fair, organized and founded in 2002 by the New Art Dealers Alliance, a not-for-profit collective of art dealers working with contemporary art. Unlike Art Basel, the Armory, or Frieze, NADA is organized by dealers, and profits are plowed back into the fair. This allows them to charge less for the fair booths, with a mildly (if still selectively) democratizing effect on its younger exhibitor base. Particularly known for their Miami art fair, which takes place at the same time as Art Basel Miami, NADA is one of the few fairs where, like at gamma galleries, you will find a highly curated assortment of younger beta galleries that might soon exhibit at Art Basel. It's a springboard to the top league and hence a great place to discover newer art. And if you like NADA, you'll like Liste Art Fair Basel: originally founded as a fair for the young galleries that didn't get into Art Basel, Liste shares a similar exhibitor base.

Collect art with unbridled fervor and build a collection that transcends the present.

Olusanya Ojikutu, Collector

SCOPE Art Show

SCOPE Art Show is a contemporary art fair held annually in New York City, Miami Beach, and Basel. It's a gamma art fair with a focus on very young galleries and emerging art, often more commercial than others. As you might expect, the participant galleries are gamma and delta outlets. Few galleries have ever made it from showing at SCOPE to showing at Art Basel. The fair is a great place to discover accessible and commercial art at affordable price points. Gamma art fairs usually accept any gallery that applies, as their main goal is to sell booths.

Discover a niche, such as a lesser-known movement, a region, or a technique that strongly piques your interest, and become an expert in that particular field. Start collecting artworks that piece by piece tell the story of your passion. For me, it is Algorithmic Art.

Michael Bouhanna, NFT Specialist

7.3 Buying at Art Fairs

Buying at art fairs is not fundamentally different from buying directly from galleries. Fairs, of course, are only temporarily assembled, and prices are slightly higher than in the gallery space to cover the costs associated with the fair. This is, however, offset by the fact that you can see a huge range of art in one location. Here are a few steps for how to buy art at fairs.

7.3.1
Step 1: Before Your Visit to the Fair

Connect before the Fair

If you are interested in the work of a sought-after artist and you know that the gallery will be at the fair, make sure you reach out *before* the fair. Galleries with profitable artists sell 15% of their offers before the fair even starts. In the first few hours after the fair opens, they sell another 40% of the inventory. Because galleries can sell out fast at fairs, VIP tickets can come in handy. Art Basel now has three different categories: First Choice, VIP, and regular visitors. The first day is reserved for First Choice card holders. The second and third days of the fair are for VIP card holders, and the remaining days are open to the public. Owners of alpha and most beta galleries usually leave once the fair opens to the public because they know that they won't make any more sales.

Once you start collecting art, challenge yourself to dream big, consistently nourish your passion and desire for art, and expand through it.
Hayat Jmammou, Collector

How Do You Get a VIP Ticket?

VIP tickets are limited to a certain number per gallery at alpha and most beta art fairs. Usually, galleries send their list of VIP ticket recipients to the fair management, who will then issue the tickets. As would be expected, Art Basel's VIP database identifies all the best buyers in the world because the fair is populated by the best galleries. If you don't have connections to a gallery or to the fair management, it will be hard to get a VIP ticket for an alpha art fair. Sponsors or press also get tickets, and you may be able to find connections through them. Historically, art advisors have discreetly passed tickets around among themselves, but Art Basel and Frieze have now introduced digital cards via a personalized app, which prevents this type of sharing of tickets. TEFAF has yet to clamp down on this practice, so if you have a friend with a ticket, you can always ask them to give it to you. A VIP ticket usually admits two.

Look at as much art as possible, preferably in person. And buy what you love, while trying to stay within a budget that is realistic for you. There are stunning and amazing artworks available at every price point. Buy art as an investment only if you have a high tolerance for risk. Shelley & Philip Aarons, Collectors

Although there are no formal partnerships in place, VIP passes to alpha fairs usually give you free access to beta and gamma fairs running concurrently, and the beta and gamma fairs will be happy to extend their hospitality to such visitors. Sadly, this arrangement is not reciprocal: VIP tickets for the peripheral beta and gamma fairs will not give you access to Art Basel.

Never buy the postcard version of the thing you really want.
Bill Powers, Gallerist

Plan Your Day Right

Whenever an alpha fair takes place, beta and gamma fairs will set up camp at the same time in the same city and often close to the alpha fair. I call these satellite fairs. These fairs are a great source of new talent, and price points at beta and gamma fairs are much lower than at alpha fairs.
As an example, the following graphic shows all the fairs that took place during the Art Basel Miami week. The circle shows Art Basel Miami Beach, and the boxes represent twenty satellite fairs, all beta and gamma fairs, which are running at the same time to take advantage of the fact that art has

come to town. Other alpha fairs—Frieze in London or New York, for example—invite a similar incursion of satellite outlets. In order to plan your day right, you should decide, before you go, which fairs you will visit. For me, in Miami, it's always Art Basel, NADA, Untitled, and SCOPE—as you can see, a variety of alpha, beta, and gamma fairs. Why not more? Simply because I get overwhelmed with the amount of art I can digest. Over the course of three days, visiting two to four fairs is absolutely enough.

Educate yourself; art fairs, gallery and museum exhibitions, and auction previews are ideal forums. Get independent advice!
Elizabeth von Habsburg, Appraiser

ART FAIRS IN MIAMI DURING ART BASEL

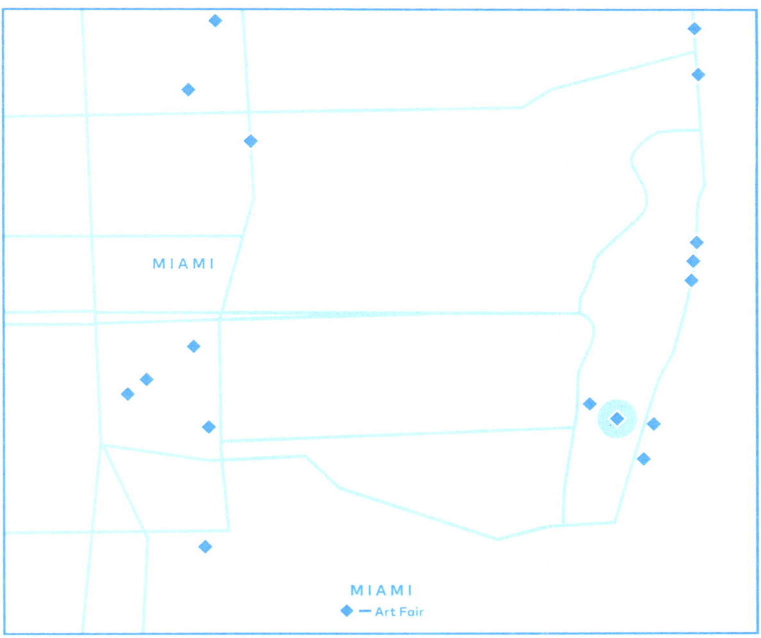

7·3·2

Step 2: Walking the Fair

Once you are at the fair, the first thing you should do is take a look at the floor map. The floor map helps you to identify the power play that is taking place and identify the foremost galleries exhibiting. As a rule, the closer a gallery is to an alpha gallery, the higher its prestige. Positions of alpha galleries at art fairs are fixed unless alpha galleries request otherwise. If a beta gallery requests a move somewhere else, they may or may not be lucky, as the fair needs to manage the requests of all beta galleries that are fighting for locations closest to the alpha galleries. To illustrate this, let's look at three floor maps.

Buy what you love, but make sure it has potential, because if it goes down in value, you will love it a lot less. David Mugrabi, Collector

Art Basel, Basel

On this floor map, you can see that all four main alpha galleries are present. They are all on the ground floor, positioned around the center lobby. These are the prime spots. Participating at Art Basel in Basel is a considerable stamp of approval. But being on the ground floor is the ultimate goal. The closer a gallery is to the alpha galleries, the higher their status. Given the profile of Art Basel, the second floor has its fair share of distinguished galleries, but a heat map of top buyers on the first VIP day would undoubtedly find traffic concentrated around the four alpha galleries.

Matthew 6:19–21 (KJV): "Lay not up for yourselves treasures upon earth, where moth and rust doth corrupt and where thieves break through and steal: but lay up for yourselves treasures in heaven . . . for where your treasure is, there will your heart be also." Collect what you want; don't get too attached. You can't take anything with you. Akili Tommasino, Curator

ART BASEL, BASEL, FLOOR PLAN

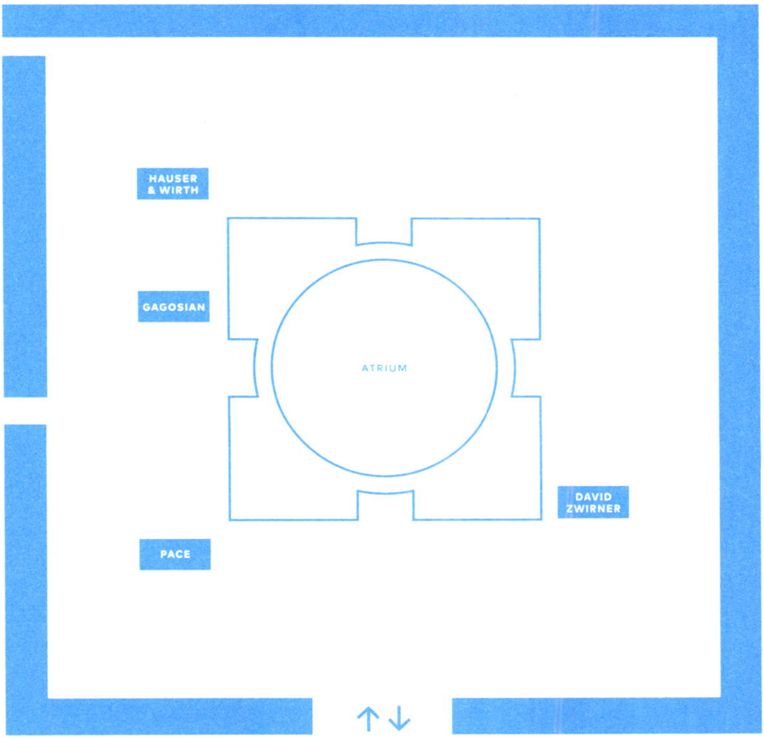

SOURCE: ARTBASEL.COM

Frieze, London

The floor map of Frieze, London, another alpha art fair, is equally interesting. Gagosian, an alpha gallery, welcomes each visitor directly at the entrance, clearly the most prominent place. Everyone needs to pass by there. Two of the other four alpha galleries are directly next to each other. Hauser & Wirth is a bit off, however, situated next to Marian Goodman, another powerhouse gallery. This layout suggests that the fair organizers wanted to create

> **Discover what excites you and then ask why—before you buy.**
> Spring McManus, Advisor

three main hubs at the fair, and, I would suggest, also wanted to drive traffic through the left-hand side, where these most powerful exhibitors are. It looks as though the right-hand side is reserved for less prominent galleries.

FRIEZE, LONDON, FLOOR PLAN

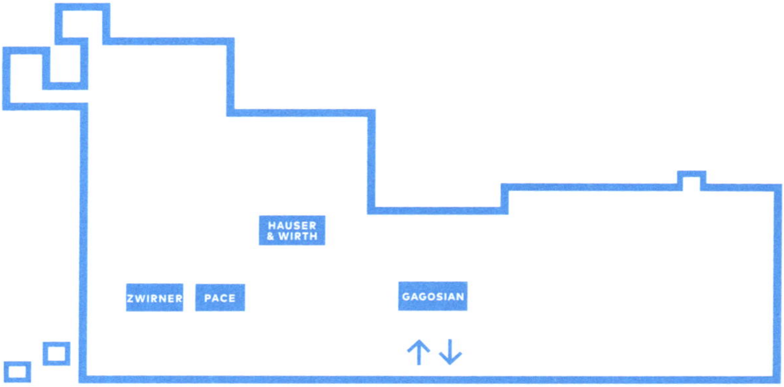

SOURCE: FRIEZE.COM

Art Basel, Miami

The Miami edition of Art Basel centers Pace, David Zwirner, and Gagosian around the same square that hosts the oyster bar and champagne. The other square, further to the right, only serves bread and water. It's hard to devise a more effective display of status than this.

What is also interesting to see is that each fair is split up into different sections, usually coded by color. While this is not obvious when visiting the fair and walking through the aisles, the colors indicate which sites galleries can apply for. These sections vary from fair to fair, but across all three classification types, there is always one main section, a second for young and upcoming galleries (younger than five years), a third for solo booths showing only one artist, and, finally, one section for large-scale

Don't start collecting art if you think you can stop.
Dani Levinas, Collector

installations (Art Basel Unlimited, for example). Interestingly, these alternative sections are usually far removed from the core section. At Art Basel they are tucked in the corners; at Frieze, they are to the far right when entering the fair.

ART BASEL, MIAMI, FLOOR PLAN

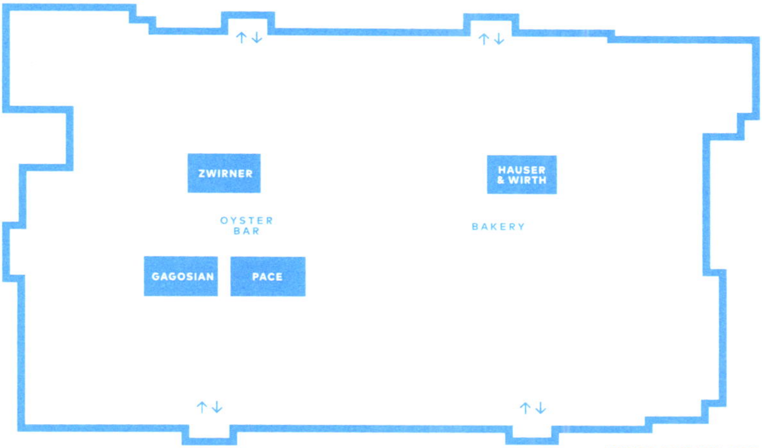

SOURCE: ARTBASEL.COM

7·3·3
Step 3: Buying at the Fair

Fairs are often not the ideal place to buy, and definitely not the place to hone unpracticed negotiating skills. Prices are often at the higher end, making it tough to get a good deal. Gallerists need to cover their costs, which are high for fair attendance—travel, staff, insurance, and transportation all make it hard to break even. A cool head is everything at fairs, as fairs present a short window for deal-making, and the

Collectors look, and look, and look at art. If you find an artist you like, look at many examples of their work. It can blur together, so take notes. Pay attention to the artists you still think about months later.

Sara Fitzmaurice, PR Expert

competitive environment is not dissimilar to an auction salesroom. Do some investigation before purchasing. What type of artist are you looking at? A superstar or a vanity artist? Is the price point okay? What are the auction results? What type of gallery is it? Everything that I have described in the Galleries chapter also applies here.

> **Buy with a focus or theme in mind to create a larger narrative.**
> Irene Kim, Collector

One way that you can get the best out of an art fair: There may be some advantage to waiting for the last hours before the fair closes. If the gallerist hasn't sold the work, she might be open to a discount, particularly if the work is large and the gallerist is persuaded by avoiding the transportation costs back to her home country.

7·3·4 Dos and Don'ts

Dos:

- **Plan ahead.**
- **Visit the educational program. Every alpha fair offers interesting talks.**
- **Revisit a work you liked on the last day and make an offer. You might be able to get a discount if the work didn't sell.**
- **Network. Fairs are a great place to network with gallerists and other collectors.**

Don'ts

- **Don't just go to the main fair—visit beta and gamma fairs as well.**
- **Don't expect to engage in long conversations on VIP days. Dealers need to sell on these days. Don't be surprised if they cut you short and move on fast to someone else.**
- **Don't buy on impulse. Do the same sober research you would do under normal circumstances, and remember that fairs are not ready sources for discounts.**

Case Study

TOURIA EL GLAOUI—PUTTING AFRICAN ART IN THE SPOTLIGHT

One of the most exciting international art fairs in the world is the 1-54 Contemporary African Art Fair, the first and only international fair dedicated to contemporary art from Africa and its diaspora. The 1-54 fair, which has three annual editions, in London, New York, and Marrakesh, and a pop-up exhibition in Paris, is named after the fifty-four nations that make up the African continent.

The fair was founded in 2013 in London by Touria El Glaoui, the daughter of the renowned contemporary Moroccan artist Hassan El Glaoui. Born and raised in Morocco, Touria El Glaoui holds an MBA in Strategic Management and International Business from Pace University, New York. She began her career in the banking industry in New York before working between London, various African countries, and the Middle East.

It was on these travels to Africa that she came up with the idea to start a fair. "I was mesmerized by the work I would see in those countries. I was always wondering why there was absolutely no trace of these fantastic artists I was seeing, either in Europe, where I was living, or in the US, where I was working a lot. It was like living in a parallel world where I was seeing amazing, fantastic, blow-my-mind type of art, and nobody was paying attention."

With an emphasis on contemporary art from Africa and the African diaspora, 1-54 has swiftly become an important specialist beta art fair that will continue to play a prominent role in the art-world calendar. Not only does it show some of the most exciting contemporary art in the world, but it has also developed a critical economic function, raising considerable sums of money through sponsorship, fundraising, grant writing, and the formation of solid partnerships with big-name organizations, corporate sponsors, and educational institutions across Europe and Africa.

For El Glaoui, it is the legacy of the show that matters. "It's the passion that makes me continue, as well as the impact we have on the artists and their careers. Also, galleries tell us we've changed their lives, so if we can help them continue what they are doing, we will."

1-54 has had a very constructive impact on the lives of artists and galleries. As a collector and a professional observer of the market, I particularly like the fair. It's professionally organized, it has a unique differentiation factor from other fairs, and it's led by a visionary founder with a true vocation. Collectors interested either in art emerging from Africa and the African diaspora or in using art collecting as a way of supporting the wider equality agenda would do well to include a trip here.

ADVICE

Viewing as much art as possible is important in developing your eye as a collector. Visit galleries, art fairs and museums regularly, and arrange studio visits to meet artists when you can. Nowadays, we also have the internet at our fingertips, so be curious! Engage with art scenes in other parts of the world and make use of it to further educate yourself.

8
Auction Houses

—Getting the Best Deals without Overpaying

Auction houses are a key selling and buying platform in the art world. Christie's and Sotheby's are the world's biggest auction brands, names known beyond the trade by mainstream buyers and even to those who do not buy at all. But auction houses have a difficult relationship with artists and gallerists. In no other place in the art world is the connection between money and art so visible.

8.1 Overview and Classification

Auction houses account for roughly 50% of the global art trade. The first auction houses were founded in the eighteenth century, and up until the 1970s, their main clients were art dealers. In the past forty to fifty years, however, auction houses have opened up to a general audience. Today, professional and nonprofessional art buyers bid alongside and, of course, against each other.

Focus on artists and works you are drawn to and love, as opposed to current trends that will come and go quickly.
Sophia Penske, Advisor

Auction houses have two main revenue streams: public auctions (70%) and private sales (30%). At public auctions, the auction house earns two sets of commissions, both paid as a percentage of the hammer price (the price on which the auctioneer's hammer falls). The buyer pays a buyer's premium of 10% to 30% of the hammer price, and the seller pays a seller's commission, which varies between 5% and 25% of the hammer price. In other words, when a painting sells at an auction for \$1 million, the buyer will have to pay \$1.2 million to the auction house and the seller will receive only \$800,000, with \$400,000 going to the auction house for facilitating the transaction. To many, this sounds like a huge amount, and they might think that in an efficient and liquid market, the intermediary wouldn't be able to take such a high commission for facilitating a deal. However, in the art world, auction houses take on a critical role by providing the platform to sell, identifying customers, researching provenance, and lending credibility to the authenticity of the work. The other advantage of an auction house lies in its unpredictability. A feverish auction-room atmosphere is a thrilling bit of theater in itself, and a bidding war between two determined

Don't buy the hype.
Simon Fisher, Art Tech Founder

parties can produce a better result for the seller than any other means.

Sometimes buyers prefer to avoid public auction and sell privately, which auction houses are also happy to arrange. Commissions may be lower than in public auctions and, in general, need to be agreed upon in advance. Each deal is subject to negotiated arrangements, with no fixed commission as standard. It's interesting to see that private sales arranged through auction houses have recently increased and show every sign of continuing to increase as sellers exercise the option of selling their works without too much public attention, not least to avoid the appearance of flipping. Even works that are put into public auctions have often been offered privately before.

There are roughly 1,400 auction houses in the world. They can be classified into four groups, followed by their description:

- **Alpha: 2**
- **Beta: 5**
- **Gamma: 300**
- **Delta: 1,100**

AUCTION HOUSE BREAKDOWN

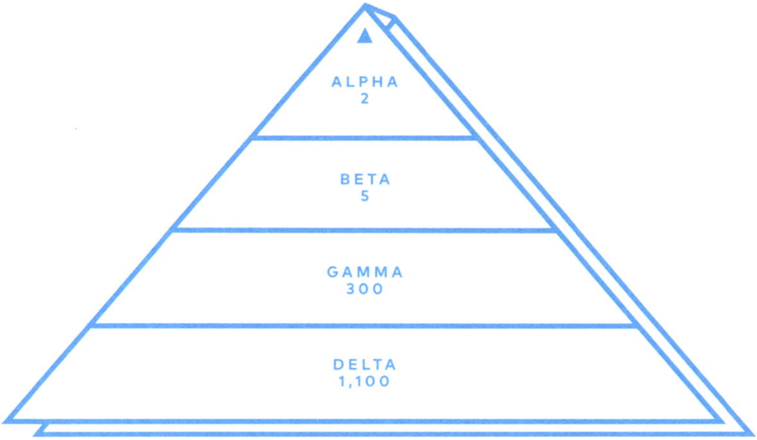

Alpha

There are only two alpha auction houses: Christie's and Sotheby's. These two names own roughly 40% of the global auction market. They have a global footprint with offices around the world. They are strong in all different sectors of the market and regularly achieve record prices for the artists they offer. Competition between Christie's and Sotheby's is fierce, as they are both fighting for the best collections to be sold by their institutions. It's also very common for them to exchange key staff, with many auction experts switching from one to the other and back again. Annual revenues of alpha auction houses are around $8 billion.

Buy from your heart. Buy what you like and not what someone else thinks will go up in value. The value may not be monetary.
William Lim, Collector

Beta

The five beta auction houses are the extended top list: Poly and Guardian in China, Heritage Auctions, Bonhams, and Phillips. These five also have an international presence, although not as extensive as the alpha auction houses. They often focus on only one sector of the art market. Revenues of beta auction houses are around the $1 billion mark—considerably less than that of Christie's and Sotheby's.

Gamma

Gamma auction houses don't have a strong international footprint. They are national or local stars and have neither international brand recognition nor international customers. Examples are Artcurial in France, Dorotheum in Austria, and Grisebach in Germany. There are around three hundred gamma auction houses, with revenues somewhere around $40 million to $100 million.

Sleep on it. Sandy Heller, Advisor

Delta

Delta auction houses are local auctions, with no national or international reach. Their average price points are much lower, and they almost never hit record prices. There are around 1,100 delta auction houses, including Kornfeld or Koller in Switzerland. Delta auction houses don't rise above the $40 million revenue mark.

8.2 Key Auction Houses

As with the gallery industry, a few players attract most of the attention and generate the highest revenue, while the rest follow at a considerable distance. Auction houses to take notice of include:

Sotheby's

In 2022 Sotheby's total sales were around $8 billion, a sharp increase on their prepandemic 2019 revenue of $4.8 billion. Revenues in 2022 were divided between $6.8 billion in auctioned art sales and roughly $1.1 billion in private sales. With more than six hundred auctions annually and selling offices in twelve cities, plus sixty-nine different departments ranging from Wine & Spirits to English Furniture, Sotheby's has a global footprint and is active in all different forms of collectibles.

Christie's

The alpha counterpart and rival to Sotheby's is Christie's, which shows a slightly higher turnover for 2022 with $8.4 billion. This success was propelled by single-owner-collection sales, such as the Paul Allen sale, which alone brought in $1.6 billion, with five works breaking the $100 million mark. Private sales made up $1.2 billion, with the remaining $7.2 billion coming from live and online auctions. It's important to understand that while both Christie's and Sotheby's have a

Every new acquisition needs to hurt and feel like it's the last missing piece in the puzzle. Collecting is a constant prioritization.

Johanna & Friedrich Gräfling, Collectors

lot of departments, the bulk of earnings ($6.2 billion) comes from their art sales. Luxury goods, an emerging category that includes handbags, sneakers, watches, and wine, and has proven to be a key entry point for millennial buyers, came in second, earning the company $988 million.

Explore editions! It's a great way to start a collection with leading artists at a lower cost.
Louise Hamlin, Advisor

A breakdown by buyer location is similar to that of Sotheby's, with buyers from the Americas accounting for about 40% of the house's total revenue, while buyers from Europe, the Middle East, and Africa make up 34% of sales. The Asia-Pacific region accounts for only 10% of buyer spending.

Phillips

Phillips is the leader in the beta group, with revenues of a little more than $1 billion. A British auction house, their focus is on contemporary and modern art. Headquartered in London and New York and owned by Russians, Phillips has long been a more boutique auction house with a more narrow focus than the alpha houses.

Poly

With sales turnover of roughly $1 billion, Poly is also a beta auction house and China's leader in fine art. Most sales take place in Beijing, with a further 5% in Hong Kong. Chinese auction houses are not permitted by law to do private sales or "nonauction sales."

Grisebach

Grisebach is Germany's leading player and a gamma auction house. With revenues of $100 million annually, they cater to a more national audience and sell mostly national artists. You will find a similar focus within other national auction houses, for example, France's Artcurial.

Karl & Faber

Karl & Faber, based in Munich, is a delta auction house. They cater to a local audience but have strong ties to national artists, and the fantastic team sells their work at attractive prices.

8.3 Buying through Auction Houses—How to Find the Best Deals

Buying from auctions is very different than buying from galleries. The auction format is pressurized, since you are in immediate competition with other bidders. There are a few things to consider when buying at auctions.

8·3·1 Step 1: Before You Bid

If you are looking for artists who have an existing secondary market, look at auctions. A good way to identify upcoming lots is via LiveArt or Invaluable.com, which you can use to set alerts by auction house or by artist name. Buying a particular artist's work at auction is in some respects simpler than buying in galleries, as the auction house is self-selecting: you simply bid wherever the work is offered. Before you can bid at an auction, you must register with an auction house to approve your credit-worthiness. Registration is usually straightforward and quick, but it is important to do this before bidding on your lot begins.

Just relax. You don't have to have everything. Danny First, Collector

There are a few terms that you should familiarize yourself with before bidding at an auction.

Guarantees
Auction houses have two main challenges: finding great works to sell and then selling them. Clearly, a common risk when selling at auction is the failure to sell. With fierce competition between houses at the top end of the market, they need to offer incentives to sellers to persuade them to consign works. That's why they offer guarantees, which hedge against the seller's risk of failure to sell. Essentially, an auction house guarantee is an agreement between the

seller and the auction house. The seller agrees to consign a work on the condition that the auction house guarantees a minimum price to be paid to the seller—regardless of whether or not the lot sells.

If it then sells for less than the guarantee, the auction house or a third party steps in to ensure the seller receives the guaranteed price. Today, 50–80% of the lots at major auctions at Christie's and Sotheby's are backed with guarantees, identified by asterisks behind the offer in the catalogue.

Only buy works of quality and value, and what you will love to live with. Linda Silverman, Advisor

Two types of guarantee are most common: a guarantee by the auction house, under which the auction house underwrites the lot, and a third-party guarantee, under which a third party underwrites the lot. The guarantor receives a fee and is given a share of the upside if bidding exceeds the guaranteed price.

There are three main reasons for offering guarantees. First, auction houses use this tool to attract customers: if a seller wants to offer her work at auction but fears that the work might yield a lower price, she will go for the auction house that offers her a guaranteed price. Second, if auction houses partner with a third party to secure the guarantee, this mitigates their risk if the work does not sell. And finally, guaranteed buyers who commit to buying the work early will increase the auction house's sell-through rate (the success rate of works offered vs. works sold), which is a key factor in convincing prospective clients to consign their work with these auction houses.

Personal friendships with advisors, artists, curators, collectors, dealers, and gallerists offer invaluable perspectives on contemporary art and insider information that others may not have access to. It is crucial to get to know several good gallerists who represent the artists you are trying to collect. Karen Levy, Collector

Estimates

Estimates are what an auction house expert believes the work will fetch. They base their decisions on current prices in the primary market, recent sales of this artist at auctions of similar works, and their own expert judgment. Sometimes estimates are on the low side to escalate bidding. You will always find estimates next to the works in an auction catalogue or on the website.

Hammer Price

The hammer price is the price of the winning bid, before fees and taxes are added.

Sale Price

The sale price is the hammer price plus the buyer's premium.

Reserve Price

The reserve price is the lowest price a seller and auction house have agreed the piece can sell for, which may equal but not exceed the low estimate. If the work fails to reach the reserve price, it will be bought in, or BI, which means that it returns unsold to the owner.

8·3·2
Step 2: Bidding

You have several ways of bidding at your disposal. If you decide to attend in person, you will first need to register. When you arrive at the auction, you will need to confirm your attendance, and you will be handed a paddle, a numbered board with which you identify yourself to the auctioneer and which you raise when you want to bid. If you can't make it to the auction, you can bid online. Some auction houses have their own app, but others, particularly gamma and delta houses, partner with Invaluable.com, which provides them with the auction-house-bidding technology. Invaluable has a user-friendly interface, and it takes only seconds to register as a buyer. Another alternative, though now less frequent, is bidding via phone. Finally, you can provide an absentee bid with the auctioneer, which indicates your specified limit for the work, and the auctioneer will bid on your behalf.

8·3·3

Step 3: After the Auction

If you won the auction, your credit card will be charged, plus the buyer's premium and tax. Once paid, you can collect the work in person, or it will be shipped to you at your expense. If you didn't win the auction, the auction house will reach out to you if any new works by the same artist are coming up for sale. Pro tip: Works that didn't sell (bought in) will often be sold after the auction. Just approach the auction house with an offer. If your offer is just below the low estimate of the work, the chances are good that you will get it.

Don't compare everything you are looking at to the greatest works you have come across.
Alexander S. C. Rower, Collector

8·3·4

Buying from Auctions vs. Galleries

If you want to buy an artist with a presence on the secondary market, you have the option of approaching the gallery or, assuming a former buyer is reselling, buying from an auction. If you are wondering which is better, I suggest here some pros and cons for buying at an auction compared to a gallery.

Pros

- **Access: In general, buying at auction is a good way to get works that you can't buy in the primary market because the gallery wants to sell only to certain collectors.**
- **Good deals: Sometimes prices at auction are cheaper than galleries. I have seen a work by artist Diego Velázquez offered for $14 million at an art fair. The same work was bought by the dealer at Bonhams in London for $4.7 million only a year earlier.**
- **Authenticity: Auction houses check the work's authenticity for you, so you can be fairly sure that the work you are buying is real.**

Cons

- Costs: You are paying the buyer's premium, which is a hefty markup of up to 30%.
- Timeline: Auctions are organized according to the sales calendar, with evening sales being the highlight and day sales reserved for the less spectacular works. This means your schedule is controlled by auction calendars as opposed to walking into a gallery and buying on the spot. You are also, of course, dependent on someone choosing to resell, a factor that may require you to bide your time and watch the market.
- Overpaying: It's all too easy to get caught up in the heat of the auction and overpay for a work. Playful auctioneers or chandelier bidding, a practice in which the auctioneer pretends to spot bids in the salesroom when in reality there are no such bids, can easily drive up prices.

8·3·5 Dos and Don'ts

Dos

- Do your homework. Scan the market and all platforms before you bid on an artwork.
- Look at past prices of your artist to get an idea of what the real market value is.
- Set a limit that you won't exceed, no matter how heated the activity is in the salesroom.

Don'ts

- Don't exceed your limit.
- Don't forget that you will need to pay the buyer's premium on top of the hammer price.
- Don't arrive at the last minute if you are a new bidder. You will need to register.

8.4 Selling through Auctions

At some point, you might like to resell your artwork, or you may have heard that an artist whose work you own is in high demand. This is what you need to think about if you want to sell art through an auction house.

8·4·1 Step 1: Check the Demand

If you are not offering a superstar or mature/emerging artist, the chances are low that any auction house will be interested. Auction houses only include works in their auctions that they are able to sell. You can check if there is demand by searching for your artist. If there are no auction results or no upcoming lots, there is probably no demand, so it's not worth reaching out to them.

8·4·2 Step 2: Identify the Best Auction House

If you are in the fortunate position that your artist has some recent sales results and also some upcoming lots—congratulations! To find the right auction house for your work, search which houses have offered works by your artist in the past and what prices they achieved. While Christie's and Sotheby's clearly have the largest reach and the biggest audience, this doesn't necessarily mean that they get the highest prices for your work. If you sell an emerging German artist who has received a lot of hype in Germany recently, your best bet might be to offer it through a German gamma auction house, as they have the right collector base for it. If you are in the lucky position of selling a superstar artist, you will probably want to work with an alpha auction house, as they have the marketing budget to promote the work. Do be aware that the whole auction house process can take from one to three months, so you need to be in a position to wait for your money.

8·4·3
Step 3: Negotiate the Deal

If you have identified an auction house that has sold your artist in the past, or perhaps even two houses, reach out via email to the appropriate department. Include a photo of the work you would like to sell and any documentation, such as invoices or catalogue entries, as well as dimensions, the location of the work, and who owns the work. This will make it easy for the specialist at the auction house to reply with a firm statement if they are interested. There is no fee for this response.

Focus on a medium you are passionate about. Try to get it as tied as possible to one line of collecting.
Mario Cader-Frech, Collector

If you receive more than one offer from auction houses interested in your work, you should consider the following:

- **Estimate: Which auction house has set the lowest/highest estimate for your work? Where has the auction house set the low estimate for your work?**
- **Guarantee: If your work is in demand, the auction house might offer you a guarantee. This lowers your risk.**
- **Costs: Sellers pay a seller's commission, which is usually between 5% and 20%. You might be able to negotiate this, so ask for the deal terms rather than agreeing on the assumption that it's a standard fee. Also ask about taxes—you don't want any nasty surprises when the work is sold.**
- **Marketing: How will the auction house market the sale? Will it promote your work online? Will there be a big image in the catalogue, or a small thumbnail?**
- **Competition: Will there be comparable works in the auction? Too many might undermine your work.**

▸ **Shipping: Who pays for the shipping to get the work to the auction?**
▸ **Timing: In which auction will your work be included?**

8·4·4

Selling through Auctions vs. Galleries

When you are selling a work, you have the option to sell through galleries or auction houses, and as with buying, you will no doubt ask yourself which one is better. Here are some pros and cons for selling at an auction vs. through a gallery.

Pros

▸ **Demand: Auctions might have existing demand for an artist if they have previously sold her work.**
▸ **Payment: Auction houses usually pay within thirty-five days. Unlike galleries, you can be confident that funds will arrive shortly after the sale. With galleries, terms and conditions are less clear-cut and far less rigorously enforced, and the work may have sold but the gallerist may not have been paid.**
▸ **Marketing: Auction houses, or more accurately the drama of the salesroom, create a sense of urgency. our work will have the attention of several buyers in that one moment, which can fuel bidding and drive prices up.**
▸ **Transparency: Selling at auction is transparent because you will know the price the buyer has paid. With galleries, depending on your arrangement with them, the actual sale price is often undisclosed, even to you as the seller.**

Cons

▸ **Timing: The auction calendar is inflexible, and a work consigned in summer might not see the salesroom until November.**
▸ **Selection: Auction houses only sell if there is a market. While gallerists can be more flexible, auction house specialists are very strict about what they offer, as they want to keep their sell-through rate high.**
▸ **Risk: Auctions are public. If your work doesn't sell, it's "burned" and will be difficult to sell for the next few years.**

You will need to keep it off the market for a few years to "rehabilitate" it.
▸ Relationship: Again, auctions are public, and the gallerist you bought the work from and the artist may react badly to learning that the work has been put into auction. This may in turn have an impact on your relationship with them, and in the worst-case scenario, the dealer may blacklist you because he considers you a flipper.

8·4·5
Dos and Don'ts

Dos

▸ If you sell your work, always approach more than one auction house. An alpha might not be your best choice.
▸ Always consider that you need to pay the seller's premium. So selling through a gallery might be a financially better option.

Don'ts

▸ Don't automatically sell through your local house. Do some research. An auction house in another country might show much more demand for the artist you are selling.
▸ Don't expect money to come in immediately. It might take several months until an auction house includes your work in their auction.

8.5 Fakes and Forgeries

Worries about fakes is one of the top concerns I hear, so I will address the issue of fakes, forgeries, and authenticity.

The good news first: fake artworks in the market is something you only need to worry about if you are buying the work of a superstar artist who is deceased and whose body of work (also called oeuvre) is not well documented. Nearly every case of fakes sold at auction have concerned works from deceased artists. Almost all the moderately priced works that you can buy at galleries, art fairs, and auction houses from living contemporary artists are going to be authentic, and I can almost guarantee that you don't need to worry about fakes.

Art-making is world-making—complexity, depth, and the unknown will offer more longevity to your collection.
Penny Rafferty, Curator

However, there are fakes at the top end of the market. Knoedler, a gallery that specialized in the secondary market, had been in business in the US for more than 160 years before it closed in 2011, selling works by Willem de Kooning, Franz Kline, Mark Rothko, and others. These are the exact types of work that could invite forgeries and should invite caution: all high-priced and all by deceased artists. Nonetheless, the gallery knowingly sold more than sixty fake artworks for millions of dollars, which they bought from another dealer who had hired a Chinese forger from Queens to produce them. Many collectors are still waiting to get their money back, and such was the notoriety that the case was portrayed in the 2020 Netflix documentary *Made You Look*. Another example is Wolfgang Beltracchi, also the subject of a Netflix documentary. Beltracchi was jailed in 2011, having created fifty forgeries, again of works from deceased and highly sought-after artists with unclear oeuvres.

Think about what interests you—what you find visually, emotionally, and intellectually compelling. Don't follow trends just because others have jumped on them, or focus only on the latest top-selling artists. Speak to artists about the artists they appreciate.
Mary Rozell, Corporate Collector

There are a few things you should consider when buying the work of deceased artists:

Newly discovered works: The best art forgers create artworks in the predominant style of the artist and pass them off as newly discovered works. They don't create masterpieces, as that would draw too much attention. They focus rather on solid works. If you are offered a newly discovered masterpiece by a deceased artist, it's almost certainly a bad forgery, especially if the seller offers it at a discounted price or claims that it was found in his grandma's garage.

Provenance: Provenance is a record of who owned a particular work from the time it left the artist's studio to the present. If you see large gaps or unclear periods, start questioning the work. Also, do not take indication of the work having been hung in a museum as evidence of authenticity. Smaller museums often don't have the manpower and money to verify authenticity, and they happily take the works unquestioned. I have even seen directors of relevant museums signing off on questionable provenances, convinced of authenticity, which later turned out to be forgeries.

Don't look at art as a financial investment. Look at art as an investment in your quality of life.
Aida Valdez, Curator

Scientific evidence: Scientific evidence means an assessment of the pigment, canvas, and stretchers to see if the materials were commercially available at the time the work was created. When you buy a house, you send in an engineer who looks at the structure and checks for things that shouldn't be there. You should do the same when buying a high-priced artwork that has a provenance with any red flags. I should say, though, that the best forgers are adept at using materials dating back to the appropriate period, so they can fool the technology.

Expert opinions: Experts are usually art historians who studied the work of an artist for many years. They have seen most of the works and are familiar with the life of the artist. Every major artist has at least some experts who claim to be authorities on the work. But be cautious: expert opinions are judgment calls, and highly subjective. Some of these experts have dubious credentials, perhaps as an expert in one artist but not in the other.

Find galleries/gallerists you trust and that are exhibiting emerging artists. Astrid Hill, Collector

Bias can also be a problem: Some experts' opinions might be compromised if they get a success fee if the sale goes through. And sometimes if an expert thinks the work is not authentic, she won't speak up because she fears being sued by the owner. Ultimately, one positive expert opinion doesn't mean that you won't find fifteen negative ones.

Certificate of authenticity: The question of authenticity really applies only to a few artworks from a selected group of artists. If you are buying works from living artists at auction houses or galleries, there is not much to worry about. However, when you buy any work, you should always do your due diligence and ask for an invoice that includes all the details, such as size, year, and material of the artwork. If any of these details are missing on the invoice, request a certificate of authenticity, a document that states the details of the artwork plus the signature of the artist. For conceptual artworks in particular, a certificate of authenticity is a must. Think of the famous banana by Maurizio Cattelan, which caused a sensation at Art Basel Miami in 2019. The work was at one point ripped off the wall and the banana eaten by a performance artist. You may reasonably think that consumption of the banana meant that the work was gone and destroyed, but no: the real value of the work lies in the certificate of authenticity. The certificate for Cattelan's work included an instruction specifying which banana is needed and at what angle to hang it. For Cattelan's work, buyers don't even receive the banana or the duct tape; they receive only the certificate. When the performance artist ripped the banana off the wall and ate it, all they had to do was put up another banana.

To create a great collection nowadays you need to have the eye/instinct to identify very early on talented artists and the courage to acquire their works before they become a trend. Timing has become more important than ever.

Eugenio Re Rebaudengo, Collector

Trust your gut and always be open to learning something new.

Jennifer Eagle, Collector

8·5·1
Dos and Don'ts

Dos

- Do your due diligence. Always ask for an invoice that includes all details when you buy a work.
- Be suspicious when you get offered an artwork by a deceased artist that is underpriced and was recently "discovered."

Don'ts

- Don't be scared of fakes of works by living artists, certainly not for any passion, vanity, or high-street artists, which have no resale value anyway. Forgers won't take the time to fake a work that has no resale value or, in most cases, one that is by a living artist.
- Don't rely solely on expert opinions. Just because the director of a museum says it's real, that isn't a guarantee. There could be fifteen other experts who think it's a fake but don't say it because they fear litigation.
- Don't buy from random dealers with no history in the market. Almost weekly, I receive an email with an offer to buy a Picasso, Monet, or Rothko—sometimes even entire collections. In most cases, the seller who approaches me is just a middleman who doesn't have access to the works or who's trying to offload fake works. Most often, they use the names as a pretext for contacting you, and then try to sell you something cheaper.

Case Study

GUILLAUME CERUTTI—TRANSITIONING CHRISTIE'S INTO A NEW AGE

Guillaume Cerutti has a long history in the art world. Originally a civil servant in the French government, he entered the commercial side of the art market and, like many employees from Christie's and Sotheby's, spent time working for both alpha houses. In 2007 he joined Sotheby's as CEO of Sotheby's France and later became deputy chairman of Sotheby's Europe. In 2015 he left Sotheby's to join Christie's as president for EMERI (Europe, Middle East, Russia, and India) and became CEO as of January 2017. Throughout this period, Christie's recorded a steady increase in sales from $5 billion in 2017 to $8 billion in 2022, their most successful year to date. Cerutti's stewardship has led the company through some art-world landmarks in the last five years, including the record-breaking $450.3 million sale of da Vinci's *Salvator Mundi* in November 2017 at Christie's New York and a private art collection handpicked by Microsoft cofounder Paul Allen, a $1.5 billion sale that marked the biggest art sale in auction history.

Although Cerutti has no background in technology, he has been at the forefront of a carefully considered negotiation with art-world tradition in his openness to innovation and technology, balanced with the need to maximize the treasured heritage that is so essential to the Christie's brand. COVID-19 only accelerated a radical but inevitable move toward technology in pursuit of new markets in all directions. The challenge of changing Christie's culture is twofold for Cerutti. On the one hand, Christie's needs to secure the top private collections that are entering the market, edging out their main competitor, Sotheby's. And on the other, they need to think beyond the traditional auction-salesroom concept and leverage the brand value to identify new revenue streams. Using a brand so deeply stamped with tradition and heritage to develop revenue streams appropriate to the twenty-first century without alienating either the original or new collector constituencies is going to require some very delicate footwork.

Christie's monetization of the hype around NFTs, however, suggests that success is in the cards. While most art-market players were never able to capitalize on it, Christie's spearheaded it, becoming one of the major platforms to sell high-priced NFTs. When Christie's sold Beeple's digital NFT piece *Everydays: The First 5000 Days* for almost $70 million, the real value lay not in the commission but in the evidence that they could tap into a new group of customers who care less and less about material wealth but prioritize experiences—customers who are comfortable with virtual-asset ownership and who simply trust that the asset is on the blockchain.

Cerutti's entrepreneurship is worth following because he isn't afraid to see traditional art-world rules through a progressive lens, striving to meet the new challenges without eradicating the value inherent in the long roots of this alpha auction house. Beyond the potential contained in technology, Cerutti also understands that the biggest potential in the art market lies in the conversion of Rookies, and he isn't afraid to use technology, powerfully united with the Christie's brand value, to attract new customer groups. It should be a formidable combination for the twenty-first century.

ADVICE

Browse, bid, and buy at online auction sales. There are opportunities there, and it's a great place for first purchases.

9
Art Advisors

—Working with Advisors

In this book we have run through the process of buying and selling artworks in galleries, at auction houses, and at art fairs. If you spend a lot of money on art, you might consider taking on the help of an expert who can do some of the groundwork for you.

9.1 Overview and Classification

Advisors support buyers in building art collections by researching, analyzing, buying, and managing their artworks. Compared to galleries and auction houses, advisors are more flexible, as they can choose from a much larger selection of artists and are not bound to the few they represent. Art advisors generally don't need physical locations, making their overhead costs far lower than those of gallerists, and their duties are light, as they don't have to undertake the broader aspects of artist support that the gallerist's role entails.

Combine courage with curiosity and the necessary cash—art collecting will lead you then to totally new insights into your own life. Rupert Keim, Auctioneer

With fewer responsibilities also come lower margins. While gallerists keep 50%, art advisors make a fraction of this. Their pricing and commission structure varies. They often either work on a retainer or take a percentage of the sales price of any work bought. It's hard to tell how many people are working as art advisors, but you could be forgiven for thinking that anyone who graduates with an art history degree or from Sotheby's Institute of Art calls themselves an art advisor. The insider term is often @gmail art advisors.

The pieces in the collection that I love the most—and that have turned out to be the most valuable—are the ones that stretched me financially to purchase. When you are pulled that strongly by a work, trust your instincts and you will ultimately be rewarded. Greg Miller, Collector

Classification of art advisors is pretty straightforward. There are two main categories:

- **Alpha: 15**
- **Beta: Everyone else**

ART ADVISORS BREAKDOWN

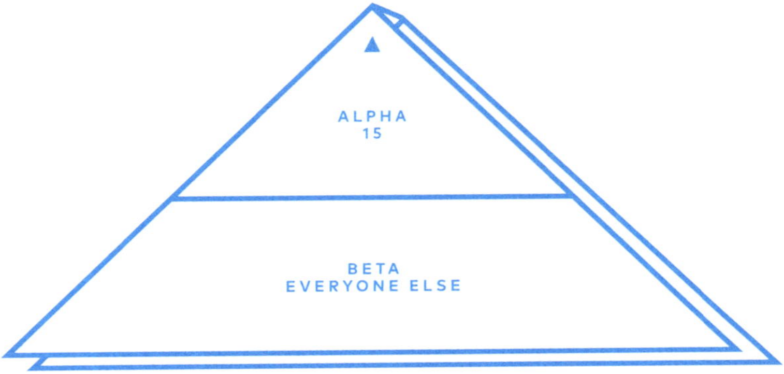

Alpha

Alpha advisors are pretty selective when it comes to taking on a new collector. They will work only with new clients with a substantial existing collection and a track record of buying art, or new buyers who are just entering the market but are willing to spend $1 million or more every year over the course of several years. These alpha advisors represent some of the most active art collectors world-wide. They work with their clients for many years and have lasting relationships, creating a solid track record in the art world. In very many cases, they previously had senior roles in galleries and auction houses. There are no more than ten to fifteen art advisors at this level.

Make certain your advisor has a good relationship with the most important dealers and access to the best artists.

Kim Heirston, Advisor

Beta

Beta art advisors are essentially everyone else. They are not selective in who they work with, they have junior roles in galleries and auction houses, and their client base is less powerful. Often, they decided against starting a gallery, deterred by the ongoing heavy costs that come with a permanent space. They want to leverage their existing network of first-time buyers and want to help rookies enter the art market. Their access to high-end artworks is limited. It's very rare for clients to work with a single beta art advisor exclusively, as their clients are usually looking for a great deal rather than building a serious art collection. The list of beta art advisors is endless, ranging from excellent to poor and from recent art-school or art-history graduates and former interns from galleries to interior architects who want to add art advisory to their services.

Look for originality—it stands the test of time.
Joe Kennedy, Gallerist

9.2 Key Art Advisors

Allan Schwartzman

Allan Schwartzman and his company Allan Schwartzman & Associates are alpha art advisors. The clients that Schwartzman advises are the savviest and most demanding billionaire collectors in the world. His record in the art world is impressive: he previously worked as chairman of Sotheby's, a company he joined after his first advisor agency was bought by Sotheby's for $85 million. His relationships to clients extend back many years, and he has worked with his clients long before his tenure at Sotheby's.

If you like free dinners, buy in the primary market.
Chum Langhorne, Collector

Amy Cappellazzo

A former partner of Schwartzman, Amy Cappellazzo is another alpha art advisor. Cappellazzo is completely open about her ambition within the art world, which is to make money. Together with her former Sotheby's coworkers Yuki Terase and Adam Chinn, she started her new art-advisory business,

Art Intelligence Global (AIG), with offices in Hong Kong and New York.

Sandy Heller

Sandy Heller is another alpha art advisor. Buying on behalf of his ten to fifteen clients, he is single-handedly responsible for roughly 5% of the art market's total turnover every year. Born and raised in New York, Heller has built up lasting relationships with his clients, which have endured over his entire career. He's been fundamental in building the mega collections of such people as Steve Cohen.

Jane Suitor

Jane Suitor is widely considered one of the leading art advisors, counting celebrities such as basketball player Kevin Love or Victoria Beckham among her clients. Suitor is known for being an active tastemaker in the art world, selling superstar artists such as Tracey Emin, George Condo, and Rashid Johnson. She also has a penchant for discovering young, emerging artists, recognizing the need to stay ahead of the curve in a rapidly evolving industry.

9.3 Finding the Right Art Advisor

Working with an art advisor sounds like a good idea if you don't want to put in the legwork. Your advisor could narrow down your search for an artist, filter results, and pre-evaluate offers, as they are more knowledgeable and connected in the art world. I would argue that most readers don't need art advisors, but I do offer some thoughts below to determine if it makes sense to hire an art advisor and how to find the right one.

All art is personal.
William Goetzmann, Collector

9·3·1

Step 1: Art Advisor: Yes or No

There are two main reasons why you might want to work with an art advisor. The first is education: new collectors appreciate the shortcut an advisor can offer. The art advisor does the research and the hard work of talking to gallerists, viewing art, going on studio visits, observing the market, going to fairs, etc. The second is access. Those artists who are in demand can only be bought by collectors with existing dealer relationships and credibility with galleries, which an advisor might be able to bring. I would argue that you don't need an advisor if you plan to spend less than $100,000 per year on art or fewer than five works per year for the next few consecutive years. If you plan to buy more valuable art or more pieces continuously over the next few years, you should consider working with an advisor.

Buy a combination of both blue-chip and emerging artists to show your unique breadth of taste and diversification of assets. And take good deals when they are presented to you by a trusted advisor—but remember, when it comes to numbers, it's art, not magic. Nick Hissom, Gallerist

9·3·2

Step 2: Select the Right Art Advisor

As there is an overload of art advisors, finding the right one can be difficult. To select one, I would suggest speaking to gallerists or artists you like and asking them if they know an art advisor who could help you navigate the art market. Another great resource is other collectors. For example, reach out to those who I quote on every page, and ask if they work with one and could put you in touch. Even if you don't know these collectors personally, you can write to

When in doubt, follow Ed Ruscha's advice: Bad art makes you say "Wow! Huh?" Good art makes you say "Huh? Wow!" Thomas Girst, Collector

them on Instagram and ask them for advice. As almost all beta art advisors are eager to find new clients, responses will follow promptly. Once you have a short list of advisors, these are the criteria I would use in selecting one:

▸ **Clients**

The profile of their existing clients is the most relevant criterion in classifying art advisors. Ask potential advisors about their clients' profiles and backgrounds, as well as how much they spend. As advisors will not reveal client names, you can only find experience-based references for advisors from the person who initially introduced you.

▸ **Longevity of relationships**

Ask about the longevity of their relationships with their clients. Collecting art seriously is a long-term game, and the ambitions of the advisor's clients and the relationship history is important. One common trait all alpha advisors have is their lasting relationships with their clients.

▸ **Track record in the art world**

The art market is a network business, and the access and knowledge that an art advisor offers come only with time. Find out how long the advisor has worked in the industry, and research which institutions the advisor has worked with. Has she worked with alpha and beta galleries or only gamma auction houses? What role did she have within these institutions? A director role at an alpha gallery or a vice president role at an alpha auction house signals that the advisor has built up a substantial network and know-how.

▸ **Price**

Art advisors use two different pricing models: a percentage of the purchase price or a retainer. In the first case, the percentage can vary between 5% and 20%. Usually, the higher the price, the lower the percentage. Since advisors often have existing relations with galleries, they might be entitled to a discount of 10% to 20%, which the advisor passes on to the collectors. So in theory, the collector is still paying no more than the gallery's retail price. Retainers are another model to compensate an art advisor. They then manage the collection, take care of loans to museums, continue to do research on existing works, and help with ad hoc consultation. Less frequent models are salaries or hourly/daily pay.

9.3.3 Dos and Don'ts

Dos

▸ **Have a written agreement with the advisor *before* you engage them. You need to be clear about their pricing and deliverables, as there are no standard practices to fall back on.**

▸ **Be aware of double-dipping. Sometimes advisors take a percentage from both the gallerist and the buyer. To prevent this from happening, always pay the gallery directly. Don't transact the purchase price via the advisor. If the purchase must be made via the advisor for some reason, always ask for invoices.**

▸ **If you buy a secondary-market work through an advisor, always ask who is between you and the seller. Often a chain of advisors is involved, and you have to fund a cut for each of them. If there are more than two parties between you and the seller, it might be a good idea to step away from the deal.**

Don'ts

▸ **Don't pay inexperienced advisors a flat fee. Most beta advisors have little knowledge. Being a postgraduate from the Sotheby's Institute of Art and hanging out at art fairs and art events or going on studio visits doesn't make them a good advisor. That said, they might be. So don't start with a flat fee, but go for the percentage model while you try them out.**

▸ **Don't try to cut out the advisor. If an advisor has done their job and pitched you an artist, don't approach the artist directly, leaving out the advisor and not paying his commission. You might get away with it once, but it's a very unfair practice and in the long run the advisor will find out.**

▸ **If a beta art advisor approaches you with an "unbelievable deal," it almost certainly isn't one. Before a beta art advisor receives it, the world's leading collectors, auction house people, and alpha advisors have seen it and were not interested.**

Case Study

AMY CAPPELLAZZO—THE ART WORLD'S AGENT OF CHANGE

Amy Cappellazzo is one the world's leading art advisors. A star in the art world, she's very open about her ambitions within it: she wants to make money. As a global player, operating in Asia and the West, she has positioned herself to be a leader moving forward.

Cappellazzo has the credibility that convinces the biggest art buyers to work with her: She co-led the Christie's contemporary art department at the age of thirty-eight. In 2014 she quit the auction house to cofound Art Agency Partners with former Sotheby's colleagues Adam Chinn and Allan Schwartzman. After Sotheby's purchased the business two years later for an estimated $85 million, she and her partners were appointed the company's chiefs of fine art, where she broke numerous art-world price records before her departure in 2021. Together with Chinn and another former Sotheby's coworker, Yuki Terase, she left to start her own art-advice business, which concentrates on the expanding Asian market. Today the business, known as Art Intelligence Global (AIG), is based between Hong Kong and New York.

Cappellazzo is exceptional because she has always seen the role of an advisor as offering potential far beyond its traditional interpretation and aims to do just that in her new venture. According to a 2014 *Vogue* interview, Cappellazzo believes that "auction houses can never fully represent a collector's interests." She adds, "What I want to do is build the best possible full-service business—not just one that makes the most money but one that can look after you the way Bessemer Trust or Guaranty Trust looked after your family."

With AIG Cappellazzo offers a service more along the lines of a traditional sports agent. She creates a client brand, positions art, promotes the artist, and negotiates contracts and product endorsements. She also plans to have a hand in organizing funds and retirement planning; in managing public relations, including websites and Twitter accounts; and in filing taxes in the various areas where artists are required to operate. Most importantly, she will interact and bargain with dealers, collectors, and museums in the same way that sports agents do with team owners, managers, and coaches.

In her undertaking to change the art market, Cappellazzo on occasion sounds like an investment banker closing a deal: "I try to make collectors feel at ease, and I also try to squeeze them when I feel they need to step up and bid. I say, 'Listen, it's like you saw the most beautiful woman in the world at a bar and you didn't ask her for a drink. What a loser!'"

With her years of experience, an extensive network, and the drive to reinterpret the role of art advisor beyond pure consulting, Cappellazzo will undoubtedly be one of the key people driving the market in the future.

ADVICE

Leave your usual orbit.

10
NFTs

—An Introduction and Overview

The year 2021 saw the rise of digital images, and 2022 saw its collapse. For a time, everyone seemed to be talking about NFTs, but few actually know what they are. While the hype around NFTs is certainly gone, I believe the technology is here to stay. That's why I want to introduce the key concepts briefly.

10.1 Introduction—The Basic Concept Explained

Contrary to common belief, NFTs are not art. Overpriced, celebrity-endorsed JPEGs that often are associated with NFTs are a form of digital art that enjoyed hype because crypto investors finally found an outlet to create a form of art investment. That bubble has burst, and the JPEGs that formed the phenomenon are now history. However, what remains is the technology that powered this hype, and it will have a future in the art world. Even traditional collectors should familiarize themselves with the basic concepts. The excitement behind NFTs, for me, is the potential they have to immediately reveal the market data behind a work you see at auction. If you want to know how many times it was traded, who owns it, and at what price they purchased it: NFT and blockchain technology power precisely this information.

Buy work you can connect with and create a vision for your collection in the process.

Jack Siebert, Collector

10·1·1 Blockchain

Although cryptocurrencies and NFTs attract all the fanfare, they would be nothing without blockchain technology. Standard definitions will tell you that a blockchain is a ledger that is digital and distributed. That means that electronic records are maintained not in a single place (such as on one Google Drive server) but spread over millions of servers. New information is added to the ledger in parcels called "blocks," which over time results in a chain of blocks draped over a network of computers that verify, approve, and store data. Think of

Collect who you are.

Frank Moore, Collector

it as a pearl chain: every time a transaction is done, another pearl is added to the chain. For those who aren't too sure of the relevance of this, the simple takeaway to take at face value is this: a blockchain is a highly secure system that doesn't allow forgery or fraudulent behavior and that cannot be hacked or adulterated because it is visible to every participant of the blockchain. This system contains a history of time-stamped, irreversible transactions, and it doesn't have a single point of input.

Mistakes are part of the growth curve when you're collecting—but mistakes are only mistakes if you've bought work you didn't like at the time because you bought with your ears and not your eyes. Graham Steele, Advisor

10·1·2
NFTs

This is where NFTs come into play. An NFT—a non-fungible token, which means nonexchangeable—is a digital record that can be used to represent an object with a value. Each is a unique digital file with its own meaning and value. The object could be physical (such as a painting, antique vase, baseball card, or ticket to a concert) or nonphysical (such as music, a video, a meet and greet with a sports star or celebrity, or a PDF or some form of digital artwork). NFTs rely on blockchain technology.

10·1·3
Metaverse

The metaverse is often mentioned in the same sentence as NFTs and blockchain. It is difficult to understand the metaverse, not least because it doesn't yet exist. According to Meta, Facebook and Instagram's parent company, "The metaverse is a set of virtual spaces where you can create and explore with other people who aren't in the same physical space as you. You'll be able to hang out with friends, work, play, learn, shop, create, and more." Currently, the metaverse is most often referred to in connection with digital real estate. Platforms such as Decentraland, Crypto Voxels, Sandbox, Mona, and Wilder World are virtual worlds where users can purchase "land" to build something on or sell later. Sotheby's, for example, has purchased land in Decentraland and has built a virtual gallery on it.

Steal it. Zachary Bahaj, Restaurateur

10·1·4

Web3

NFTs, blockchain, cryptocurrencies, the metaverse—they all define aspects of what is often referred to as Web3, another currently popular buzzword. The term is a reference to the evolution of the internet, which is currently on the cusp of its third major phase. In Web1—and here we are going back to the days of AOL—we were able to read information on the web. Now we are in Web2 and are able to read and write. However, this comes at a price: whenever you upload a file, such as your art or a song or photo, ownership of that file immediately transfers to the company that owns the platform. These companies, for example, Instagram, then monetize your content by selling your data and content to advertisers, who then feed you ads so that you purchase products from them. We accept this arrangement because the platforms allow us to upload and share our content easily and freely, and these platforms have thus become power players in

Don't rush to buy. Look, learn, think, and then start to buy. Seek advice from smart people you trust. Patronize your local museum and you will have accessto the thoughts of great curators. Know what your peers are doing but seek to form a collection that will be a unique reflection of you. Don't buy for investment, but do spend your money wisely. Always be prepared to challenge your own taste and assumptions.

Allan Schwartzman, Advisor

today's economy. Parts of the internet are now centrally controlled by a handful of big tech companies, such as Google, Meta, Amazon, and Apple. Web3 attempts to change this by creating a decentralized form of the web so that creators of art, music, and other content can own their data, as well as their own creations, in the form of digital assets. In a perfect Web3 scenario, the blockchain will maximize ownership, transparency, provenance, access, revenue streams, liquidity, patronage, and collection. For the art world, this could mean less dependency on galleries and art institutions that currently control transactions, ownership records, authentication, and relationships. In Web3, artists—not the galleries, dealers, or curators—are in control of their market. Artists decide who receives what percentage of the project, determine their relationship with the buyer, set the terms, and claim resale royalties.

Collectors who support artists at the beginning of their trajectory have the opportunity to make a real difference. Because curiosity is a form of generosity, one that is enthusiastic about sharing and exchanging knowedge and ideas, one that seeks to create and expand connections. As Albert Camus wrote: "Real generosity towards the future lies in giving all to the present."

Hans Ulrich Obrist, Curator

10.2 Benefits for Collectors

I understand that some of these terms might still sound too abstract and technical, but outlining tangible collector benefits may be helpful. Advantages for collectors include:

Unique proof of ownership

NFTs are a secure and unique proof of exclusive ownership. Essentially, the NFT authenticates, for all to see, that the collector is the owner of that artwork, and it shows all previous owners, establishing a clean provenance.

Proof of authenticity

The NFT replaces a paper certificate of authenticity. The holder can show that the item is the original piece made by the creator. This doesn't only apply to digital art but will apply to all physical art.

Transparency

The blockchain records the fact that you have purchased the NFT. It records who you bought from, who the previous owners were, and what each party paid for it. Everyone has access to the history of the work, rather like when you visit streeteasy.com (a New York City apartment purchase and rental site) and can see how much your neighbor is paying or what the previous tenant of your apartment paid.

Listen to your heart. You only regret the art that you don't buy.
Mike Steib, Art Tech Founder

Utility

Additional utility beyond simple ownership can be coded into the NFT. Value can be added by including a copy of the creator's signature, giving some form of exclusive access to the artist, or providing early notification of events hosted by them, VIP tickets, or special access. For example, some NFTs can provide access to the artist's networking and community events and discussions. Access to these exclusive benefits is lost once an NFT is sold.

A liquid asset

An NFT can be sold directly to a buyer (assuming there is a buyer, of course). This can be done anytime, without the involvement of an intermediary. The marketplace that facilitates the transaction takes a small commission, similar to the fee a credit-card company takes when their card is used.

Don't! Kenny Schachter, Collector

10.3 Benefits for Artists

The benefits for buyers are strong, as they eliminate some of the downsides of buying in the traditional art market, but artists benefit tremendously as well:

More control

NFTs give artists more power. They have more control over the determination of value, and they can see who is buying their works and receive payments immediately because the process eliminates galleries and dealers from the artist-audience relationship.

Royalties

Artists can create NFTs that are coded to allow them to receive royalties, meaning that all future resales, not just the first sale, will push a portion of the price back to the creator. Thus, if an artist sells a piece for $10,000 and ten years later it reappears on the market with an asking price of $10 million, the artist will directly benefit from that increase in value.

10.4 Summary

I think the introduction of NFTs and the various ways of using them has the potential to change the market in a way that could not be accomplished otherwise. The current convergence of digital art, crypto money, and blockchain technology will bring about a profound structural shift in the art ecosystem. Collectors won't buy if a work is not registered on the blockchain. Artists will exert more control over their work and earn royalties

We find many artists through artists that we collect.

Susan & Michael Hort, Collectors

from resales. More collectors will populate a transparent market. And the art market will become more regulated—for the better.

There are certain galleries and institutions which have almost unlimited power to make or break an artist's career. Gaining access to the "Holy Land" early on is the best way to ensure artistic success.
Sam Fraiberger, Scientist

For the artist, in the future, it is not unlikely that every artwork that leaves a studio will be registered by the artist on the blockchain, so that when it's traded, the artist not only gets royalties but also knows who the new owner is. This allows them to work more independently with less reliance on galleries to promote or authenticate their works. As a consequence, artists will earn more on every piece they sell.

With this change, there will also be a change in the power structures. Much like the entertainment industry in the 1930s, the power in the art world will shift from distribution channels (galleries) to creators (artists). However, more independence for artists will bring more responsibilities. In a world where collectors communicate directly with the artists, who will sell the works when the artist is busy creating? In order to sustain this shift, artists will need to become more entrepreneurial and learn to manage new tasks. Some will hire more staff; others will gladly work with galleries that take on the jobs of selling, promoting, placing, and supporting—roles galleries are already performing today. But the power dynamics will have shifted.

A collecting journey requires guideposts. Some of ours are: 1. We own trophies; we don't buy trophies. 2. Nothing comes into the collection that doesn't speak to the collection. 3. Acquire with your eye not your ear. Bob Rennie, Collector

Collectors will be most impacted by the development of the new art ecosystem. Given that the role of the middleman has shrunk, they will be in closer, more direct contact with artists. When every artwork is registered on the blockchain, collectors will feel more confident buying art because they will know current prices, past prices, and comparable prices. And more collectors will enter the market because information on provenance will have become clearer and more accessible, eliminating much of the historical mystique that the art industry has, to some extent, fostered. Selling artworks in the traditional market is currently very difficult and always requires a middleman. Using NFTs, the sale process is much easier and allows much faster transactions, offering an easier way to get a return on investments for those who are financially motivated or perhaps would just like to trade up.

Once you've identified the artist you'd like to collect from an aesthetic or commercial point of view, if you can't afford the painting, buy the drawing. If you can't afford the drawing, buy the print. Jane Suitor, Advisor

Does this mean the art market will change entirely tomorrow and all its alpha to delta players will vanish? Definitely not, because changes in the art world take time. Furthermore, the inner sanctum of the art market will surely endure, relying as it does on established relationships. Does it mean that Picasso will be replaced by Beeple and MFA programs will mostly graduate digital artists? Also, no. Painting is not dead, and digital art as a medium will continue to constitute a small share of the market. Only a few projects out of the current NFT hype are likely to make it into the top museums. Most will resume their pre-bubble relevance.

Develop your personal taste by looking, not listening. Then spend as much as you can afford to acquire the very best of what gives you genuine pleasure, and expect to enjoy it for many years. Michael Findlay, Gallerist

The advantages of NFTs and blockchain technology will contribute to a better art market, one that is fairer, more equal, and more democratic. A market that is more inviting, less exclusive, and more transparent, converting a large number of new visitors into buyers who purchase art. Art institutions can benefit tremendously from the new capabilities that NFTs and their underlying technologies give us by better engaging their communities and giving them ownership through participation and involvement in governance.

Obviously, not everyone is excited about the prospect of change in the art industry. But the writing is on the wall. Nostradamus-like predictions of the gradual decline of the traditional art world into antiquity may be slightly premature. I believe we are simply entering a new era. For collectors like you, it will be fascinating to follow this development.

Eyes, not ears. Studio visits. Footwork. Study. Love. Fun.

Tiffany Zabludowicz, Curator

Case Study

PABLO RODRIGUEZ-FRAILE—PATRON OF DIGITAL ART

Pablo Rodriguez-Fraile is a blockchain investor and an art collector who owns the most significant digital-art collection worldwide. Rodriguez-Fraile also launched Aorist, a cultural institution bringing digital art to global cultural events. Those who went to Art Basel Miami in the past few years will have seen Aorist's large-scale exhibitions at the Faena beach.

In the hype around NFTs, Rodriguez-Fraile invented a new type of collector in the digital-art patron. As an early adopter of NFTs, his collection of crypto art now contains more than two thousand NFTs, including thirty works by Beeple, seventy works by Pak, and others by Mad Dog Jones and Trevor Jones. His patronage has thus played a role of considerable cultural significance in the expansionist process of embedding a digital-art world, but Rodriguez-Fraile has also been highly successful from an investment viewpoint: in October 2020 Rodriguez-Fraile bought a ten-second Beeple video clip for $66,000, which he sold in March 2021 for $6.6 million.

Making money, however, is not the reason why Rodriguez-Fraile is so active in the digital space, nor is it why I wanted to interview him. He has a deep understanding of what it means to collect art and live with it, whether digital or otherwise. In his collection at his Miami home that he shares with his wife, Desiree Casoni, digital art coexists comfortably with painting and sculpture. In the entryway, Elizabeth Peyton's portrait of David Bowie hangs opposite Beeple's depiction of a nude, fleshy Buzz Lightyear straddling a Jeff Koons balloon dog.

While many NFT buyers were in it for the money, he wasn't. "I want to make sure there is always a spot for those who are fundamentally behind the art and the culture, rather than the promise of making money." In this spirit, Rodriguez-Fraile is paving the way for more collectors to enter the digital space, making digital art more accessible through Aorist. In our interview, he explains why he believes so strongly in digital art. For Rodriguez-Fraile, while the traditional art market has not frequently created strong personal relationships between artist and collector, digital art has produced more direct relationships as part of its evolution: "In the traditional space, the direct contact is much rarer because there are more steps along the way to find a connection with the artist. When it comes to digital art, I have a relationship with most artists I collect, helping them with their career: assisting with PR communications, introducing them to collectors, fulfilling the roles that other institutions play in the traditional art world."

I love seeing the digital space developing and believe it's a great area for collectors who want to help their artists build a legacy and move the space forward. As Rodriguez-Fraile says, "The relationships we have with these digital artists are not merely transactional. Seeing my artists excited gives me incredible joy and pleasure."

ADVICE

Spend the time and put in the effort to understand the artist, the intentions, and the sophistication in the art you are seeing.

Appendix

—Author's Note and Participants

Author's Note

The book you just read is one of the most important I have written because it gets to the core of the art world's problems, and specifically one I have been trying to fight for so long: there are not enough buyers. I wrote this book in the hope that some of my readers will start buying one or two art pieces after having read it. With your art purchase, you will support artists and gallerists who are dear to my heart. I truly believe that as a society we will grow if more people buy art and live with it in their homes.

It took me a lot of talking and listening with my students and friends who were new to the art world to develop the answers to the questions they have. My PhD, my studies, and several years of practical work—altogether almost twenty years of research—went into this book. I hope that I was able to give answers to at least some of your questions. And I hope I was able to show you my deep admiration for artists and gallerists and other art-world practitioners who are working hard every day in a tough industry that shows little monetary reward.

I have talked at length about classifications of artists, advisors, galleries, art fairs, auction houses, and collectors. These classifications should help you to navigate the art market so that you know what you are buying. Does this mean that vanity artists from delta galleries create bad art? Not at all. Bad art doesn't exist, just bad investments. In fact, if you follow me on Instagram (@magnusresch) you will see that I spend most of my time at gamma art fairs, delta galleries, and with vanity artists. I take what I call responsible buying very seriously—the idea of not only buying as an investment but also as a philanthropic act. Or simply said: I buy what I like; I collect to support a community, but I never overpay.

If you liked my book, post a photo of it on Instagram and tag me. If I see your story, I will share it. I am always curious to see who is reading my book. And if you would like to talk to me directly because, for example, you have specific questions or need a second opinion on the purchase of an artwork or want to gift your partner an art-market seminar, you can book a 1:1 session with me. Simply visit magnusclass.com.

Some interviews can be watched on magnusclass.com.

Participants

Shelley and Philip Aarons
Ashley Melisse Abess
Jam Acuzar
Alexander Adler
Jongsuwat Angsuvarnsiri
Mouna Atassi
Josh Baer
Zachary Bahaj
Moran Bar-Kochva
LeRoy Bennett
Walda Besthoff
Glen Bjørnholt
Cyril Blot-Lefèvre
Bruno Bolfo
Andrea Bonaceto
Michał Borowik
Michael Bouhanna
Karen Boyer
Claire Breukel
Isabelle Bscher
Torsten Butzen
Mario Cader-Frech
Erick Calderon
Amy Cappellazzo
Sean, Lauren, and David Aaron Carpenter
Troy Carter
Guillaume Cerutti
Robert Chambers
Adam Chinn
Michael Chutko
Curtis Clarizio
Bonnie Clearwater
Kat Cohen
Sophia Cohen
Michael Cohen
G. Andrea Danese
Jeffrey Deitch
Rosa and Carlos de la Cruz
Suzanne Delehanty
Simon de Pury
Sofia Derani
Chris Dercon
Beth Rudin DeWoody
Delphine Diallo
Maurin Dietrich
John Dodelande
Diandra Donecker
Jennifer Eagle

Touria El Glaoui
Nicola Erni
Alexandre Errera
Katarina Feder
Andrea Feldman Falcione
Désiré Feuerle
Michael Findlay
Danny First
Simon Fisher
Sara Fitzmaurice
William S. Floyd
Sam Fraiberger
James Fuentes
Nichole Galicia
Viera Gaon
Denise B. Gardner
Erin Jenoa Gilbert
Thomas Girst
Marc Glimcher
Marta Gnyp
William Goetzmann
Jessica Goldman Srebnick
Loïc Gouzer
Johanna and Friedrich Gräfling
Oleg Guerrand-Hermès
Steven Guttman
George Hamilton
Louise Hamlin
Ronald Harrar
Kim Heirston
Sandy Heller
Gregor Hildebrandt
Astrid Hill
Nick Hissom
Sabrina Ho
Phyllis Hollis
Susan and Michael Hort
Kelly Huang
Anne Huntington Sharma
Nicole Ianniello
Charlie Jarvis
RF Jefferies
Hayat Jmammou
Dakis Joannou
Caspar Jopling
Erling Kagge
Peter Kahng
Rupert Keim

Joe Kennedy
Irene Kim
Vajra Kingsley
Jeremy Kost
Felix Krämer
Bernie Lagrange
Chum Langhorne
Alan Lau
Jaclyn Lavy
Cathy Leff
Dani Levinas
Barbara Levine
Karen Levy
Sylvain Levy
William Lim
Adam Lindemann
Julie Macklowe
John Marquez
Patricia Marshall
Spring McManus
George Merck
Kathryn Mikesell
Greg Miller
Frank Moore
Mills Morán
David Mugrabi
Shaun Neff
Sandra Neumann
Hans Ulrich Obrist
Olusanya Ojikutu
Larry Ossei-Mensah
Sophia Penske
Jorge M. Pérez
Ron Pizzuti
Andi Potamkin
Bill Powers
Lauren Prakke
Joshua Pulman
Howard E. Rachofsky
Penny Rafferty
Amitha Raman
Magnus Renfrew
Bob Rennie
Eugenio Re Rebaudengo
Ellie Rines
Claus Busch Risvig
Andreas Ritter
Donald Robertson
Benedict Rodenstock
Pablo Rodriguez-Fraile
Victoria Rogers
Donna Rosen

Alexander S. C. Rower
Mary Rozell
Mera and Don Rubell
Roya Sachs
Tom Sachs
Dan Sallick
Patrizia Sandretto Re Rebaudengo
Catherine and Mamadou-Abou Sarr
Kenny Schachter
Julian Schnabel
Dennis Scholl
Allan Schwartzman
Doron Sebbag
Philippe Ségalot
Alain Servais
Zeki Sever
Komal Shah
Tariku Shiferaw
Michael Shvo
Jack Siebert
Linda Silverman
Stefan Simchowitz
Ryan Stanier
Graham Steele
Mike Steib
Tavares Strachan
Jane Suitor
Ed Tang
Akili Tommasino
Aida Valdez
Marlies Verhoeven Reijtenbagh
Elizabeth von Habsburg
Chris Vroom
Dorothée Wahl
Adam Weinberg
Leopold Weinberg
Rüdiger Weng
Anna Weyant
Brian Whiteley
Debi Wisch
Melissa Cowley Wolf
Doug Woodham
Ato and Tonya Wright
Teo Yang
Tiffany Zabludowicz
Heidi Zuckerman
Ryan Zurrer

Phaidon Press Limited
2 Cooperage Yard
London E15 2QR

Phaidon Press Inc.
111 Broadway
New York, NY 10006

phaidon.com

First published 2024

ISBN 978 1 83866 625 5

A CIP catalogue record for this book is available from the British Library and the Library of Congress.

Design by Karolina Rosina-Meisen, thegentletemper.com

Printed in China